DEFENDING IDEALS

DEFENDING IDEALS

WAR, DEMOCRACY, AND POLITICAL STRUGGLES

DRUCILLA CORNELL

Routledge
New York • London

Published in 2004 by
Routledge
270 Madison Avenue
New York, NY 10016
www.routledge-ny.com

Published in Great Britain by
Routledge
2 Park Square
Milton Park, Abingdon
Oxon OX1 4RN U.K.
www.routledge.co.uk

Routledge is an imprint of the Taylor & Francis Group.

Printed in the United States of America on acid-free paper.

10 9 8 7 6 5 4 3 2 1

Library of Congress Cataloging-in-Publication Data

Cornell, Drucilla.
  Defending ideals : war, democracy, and political struggles / by Drucilla Cornell.
    p. cm.
Includes bibliographical references.
ISBN 0–415–94882–7   ISBN 0–415–94883–5 (pbk.)
1. Political science—Philosophy. 2. United States—Foreign relations—2001–3.
Iraq War, 2003. 4. Human rights. 5. Women and peace. 6. Intercountry adoption. I. Title.
JA71.C598 2004
320—dc22   2003026845

Contents

Preface: Why We Need Ideals

The essays in this book defend ideals such as freedom, equality, and peace. We need ideals more than ever after September 11, 2001. This hardly seems like a controversial claim, for who would disagree with it? Both proponents *and* critics of the United States wars in Afghanistan and Iraq claimed that they defended their respective positions on the basis of ideals. To argue over ideals in politics means that we defend not only their theoretical importance, but also how they are applied in actual political situations and struggles on the ground. If the peace movement in this country is going to convince people that the ideal of peace is vitally important, it must make arguments against the Bush administration's appeals to freedom as the basis for its recent preemptive military strikes and protracted military occupations. Remember that the Bush administration said that we needed to attack Iraq because of its weapons of mass destruction and strong links to Al-Qaeda. It was only when no evidence for either could be marshaled that the discourse of freedom was deployed to shore up the legitimacy of the United States military campaign in Iraq.

So the questions arise. Does this fact alone show the infinite manipulability of ideals? Is the battle over ideals just the battle for power dressed up in fancy clothes? In this book, I do not want to argue that anyone who defended the war in Iraq from the standpoint of enduring freedom was simply insincere. Rather, I want to suggest that configurations of ideals that, for example, represent freedom and "shock and awe" as compatible are, however, flawed. We can still make judgments about competing definitions of ideals. Certain actions and practices are not compatible with respect for those ideals, even as understood as allowing for a range of interpretation. Freedom cannot be brought at the point of a gun. But not everyone appealed to ideals to defend the actions of the government of the United States. After September 11, a new discourse of political realism arose that not only justified the Bush administration's military actions in the war on terror, but also supported legislation that curtailed basic constitutional liberties in the irresponsible name of an idealized form of national security. Often cast in the guise of irresponsible liberals, idealists were thought to be horribly out of touch with post-9/11 realities, particularly the foremost need to fight terrorism.

I share the view with many progressive activists and intellectuals that steps should have been taken to bring Al-Qaeda to justice. But note the word "justice" here. Our moral outrage was based on the sense that September 11 was a crime against humanity and, for that very reason, the worst kind of injustice and human atrocity. Even in the propagandistic explanations of the Bush administration as to why "they" hate "us," we were returned to the great ideals for which the United States stands. Thus, we were told that "they" hate "us" because we are free. The cynicism of the Bush administration aside, everyone should have been called to recommit themselves to those ideals in their political response to September 11. When rage and fear seemed to demand immediate war efforts and military campaigns, we were tested in our commitment to those ideals. We continue to be tested as the war in Iraq each day takes more military and civilian lives, despite the Bush administration's proclamation in the spring of 2003 that the war was over and that we had won. Simply put, we need to reexamine our ideals precisely at a time when we are most likely to forsake them in an effort to protect ourselves against further acts of terrorism.

Respect for the rule of law as against the rule of men, whether on the national or international plane, is an indispensable political as well as legal ideal—not a wistful or naïve dream. I want to argue against those who critique the movement for peace and justice as being immature and irresponsible. We *are* responsible because we insist that, in the war against terror, we cannot controvert the ideals that, at its best, the United States has defended for over two centuries. We are the ones who are calling for a thoughtful response to September 11 that includes a rigorous examination of how we can be most effective in dismantling the transnational networks of Al-Qaeda and in preventing further acts of terrorism.

I grew up in a time when the need for security against communism led the government of the United States to curtail civil and constitutional rights within this country and to engage in grossly unjust military conflicts in the name of national security. The paranoia about communism denied us access to information, and prevented many different points of view from being heard. I was educated out of fear rather than a commitment to democratic citizenship, and I do not want to see that happen again to this generation. Political realism dominated the war against communism. Then as now, idealism was easily targeted as being out of touch with the nature of the political threat. The word "communist" was all too easily bandied about as an epithet against the leaders of the communist as well as the civil rights movement. But in the current peace and justice movement, many of us today are standing by the ideals of the civil rights movement as we criticize and protest against certain flagrantly unconstitutional provisions of the USA PATRIOT Act. Idealism is not the problem. If we vigorously debate what our commitment to ideals should mean, and if we demand that we struggle openly about their meaning, that is all to the political and moral good.

I am proud to be a member of the "60s generation," the generation most easily associated with the idealism that animated the civil rights movement and the innumerable demonstrations against the Vietnam War. I am also proud to be a feminist committed to freedom and equality. But for all that I have already said here about the importance of ideals, I do not want to discount the most important critiques of them, even as I take issue with the charge that idealists are dangerous after 9/11 because they encourage irresponsibility in the face of a real threat. There are serious criticisms of idealism that I take to heart, especially the critique that targets the danger of the idealization of ourselves and, with it, the threat of self-righteousness. Sometimes we idealize ourselves in the name of the purported moral superiority of our ideals—a superiority that can no longer be put into question because ideals have been established as the basis of how we see ourselves. Indeed, even the grandest of ideals, as soon as they are articulated and defended—even the ideal of humanity—can become exclusionary at the very moment of their defense. As many contemporary theorists and philosophers have noted, norms can normalize and set others outside the norm as abnormal or, worse yet, not within the reach of humanity. Similarly, some may want to argue that because rights can legally embed certain limited conceptions of the human being in the abstract form of the person, human rights deny the ideality of humanity and, further, that this denial remains unshakeable within a rights-based legal system. Many of us are familiar with these criticisms; they are warnings that must be heeded in the way we defend ideals as necessarily open, as never yielding once and for all a total configuration of their meaning, even when they become material forces in the world. Ideals neither emerge out of thin air nor do we simply dream them up. They are a part of our historical and social reality and, indeed, they have been critiqued as nothing more than expressions of the interests of the most powerful. These are criticisms that can never be answered once and for all. They must be taken into account as part of a complex and nuanced defense of ideals. That such a defense of ideals is possible is the burden of this book.

Drucilla Cornell

Acknowledgments

Four of these essays were originally presented as the Gilbert Ryle lectures at Trent University in Peterborough, Canada. I was grateful for the opportunity to spend four days among such a committed and thoughtful group of scholars. Their probing questions raised so many issues for me and I tried as best as I could to address them in the revisions that they inspired. Two essays, "Variegated Visions of Humanity: A Reexamination of Rawls' Law of Peoples" and "Other Family Stories: The Ethics and Politics of Transnational Adoption," were written for this volume. In the course of the lectures, many people asked me to address John Rawls' monograph *The Law of Peoples*. I added the essay in part because this book of Rawls has become so important given our current international situation, dominated as it has been by the United States' "war on terror." Because four of the essays were originally given as lectures, I tried to sound certain themes and build off material presented the night before. Some repetition necessarily results. I want to thank not only the scholars at Trent University for their careful attention and welcome criticisms, but also those who participated in other seminars, teach-ins, and colloquia where I gave versions of the original lectures.

As always, I am in the debt of those who took the time to read the revised manuscripts and give me comments. I particularly want to thank Thomas Nagel for his thoughtful criticisms on an earlier draft of the essay on John Rawls' law of peoples. I also want to thank Sara Murphy for her thoughtful comments on the original four lectures. Her editorial skill has always been invaluable to me and I am grateful to her for taking the time to read the drafts that I was endlessly presenting to her. Sara's knowledge of Freud was especially important to me in the essay on transnational adoption. My research assistant Daniel Morris devoted endless hours to working with me as we prepared the initial lectures. His erudition was an invaluable resource. His thoughtful criticisms and editorial suggestions have undoubtedly made the essays in this book much clearer than they otherwise would have been. Veena Viswanatha and Claudia Leeb, the assistants who took over from Daniel Morris, read the entire manuscript and helped to fine-tune it through hours and hours of discussion. Their help in the final preparation of the manuscript was invaluable to me. I am in their debt both for their incisive criticisms and for their editorial suggestions. Their patience in working through their suggestions helped me to take the time to work out details of my argument. I have been truly lucky to be surrounded by such intelligent young people who show all the virtues of the excellent scholars they will no doubt become.

My editor, Karen Wolny, read draft after draft of the essays and gave me comments on all these drafts. She is an old-fashioned editor in the best sense of the word. Karen shows unflagging commitment to all of her authors and we all benefit from the time and attention she gives to our manuscripts. It is an honor to work with her.

I also want to thank Larry Brassell and Irena Molitoris for providing me with the help and support I need in order to be a mother and a writer. They bring both joy and sustenance to my household. My daughter Sarita Cornell always forgives me for the time I take away from her in order to write. She shapes the way I think about the burning issues of peace and justice, since so much of what I advocate is inseparable from the world I wish for her to inherit. The entire Bryant family, Crystal and Mervin, have become part of our day-to-day lives, to the point where we think of them as family. Calvin Steven always brings support and friendship to my daughter and to myself. But one person has become a crucial ally and friend in the complex journey of mothering. I rely upon her advice, her wisdom, and her humor to help me find my way through all the complex questions and dilemmas that being a mother presents. This book is dedicated to her, Libina Bryant.

Living and Dying in Iraq: Killing Talk and the Limits of Just War   1

"Smoking Baghdad" was a special insert in the Sunday edition of *The New York Post* that came out two weeks into the invasion of Iraq. It was some 20 pages graphically depicting a city in flames. My guess is that "smoking" was meant to be a play on words, to smoke someone being a somewhat dated expression for killing. We were smoking Baghdad, literally consuming the city in flames and killing those who lived there. Interspersed with these horrifying pictures of a magnificent city being destroyed were quotes from the military strategists who planned "shock and awe." As Harlan Ullman, one of the strategists behind shock and awe, claimed, "the missiles will destroy everything that makes life in Baghdad livable." He continued, "We want them to quit; we want them not to fight . . . You take the city down . . . You have the simultaneous effect, rather like the nuclear weapons at Hiroshima—not taking days or weeks but minutes."[1]

I live in New York City and can remember only too vividly the horror of the horizon of smoke and fire that filled the New York sky on September 11, 2001. And I can remember the terrible fear that came with not knowing if there would be another attack. But the people in Baghdad did know there were going to be other attacks from the United States. Waiting day after day, night after night in fear as the search for Saddam Hussein continued. There is no way to protect against the kind of bombardment that the United States was pursuing as part of its strategy, which is of course part of the point. It is a strategy that is meant to bring out the paralysis of helplessness. The bombardment begins with no relief in sight, with nowhere to run, and nowhere to hide.

In her diaries of the first Gulf War, the artist Nuha Al-Radi describes life under the 42-day bombardment that the people of Baghdad endured in that war. She and her family lived outdoors in an orchard because the outdoors, in fact, seemed to be the safest place, as it was away from burning houses and shattering glass. "With the first bomb, Ma and Needles' windows shattered, the ones facing the river. It's a good thing their shutters were down, otherwise they could both have been badly hurt. One of poor Bingo's pups was killed in the garden by flying glass—our first war casualty."[2]

After that scare, it seemed to them safer to stay outside. The first day, electrical power went down. By the fifth day, water had become scarce. Then, toilet facilities no longer functioned. "We are now all going to the loo in the orchard, fertilizing it and saving ourselves some water which no longer flows out of the taps."[3] Water became scarcer and scarcer, until it finally ran out. "We've now been without water for one week. My hands and nails are disgusting. Everyone has a sooty face. No one bothers to look in the mirror anymore. Needles is the only one who still looks neat and clean. Raad says that in Jadiriyah they have no more day; the sky is permanently black from the smoke of the Dora refinery as it burns. It has been burning from the first day of the war. Poor Suha and Assia; how are they surviving?"[4]

Phone service was gone. The only way to know the fate of loved ones in other parts of Baghdad was to physically go there. As gas became a rare commodity, people set out on bikes, on foot, using whatever means they had to ease the anxiety they felt over not knowing whether loved ones were still alive; they desperately needed to see the faces of their loved ones. But because Baghdad had been built around a river, the bridges were crucial for these desperate trips. Despair set in when the bridges were hit.

> They have started hitting the bridges again. Jumhuriya Bridge is now apparently in three pieces. Countless industries, textile factories, flour mills, and cement plants are being hit. What do they mean when they say they are only hitting military targets? These are not military installations. As for "our aim never goes wrong" . . . who will save us from these big bullies?[5]

Nuha Al-Radi then personally went to see the Jumhuriya Bridge and movingly tells of the experience. "I saw the Jumhuriya Bridge today. It's very sad to see a bombed bridge. A murderous action, for it destroys a link. Everyone is very strangely affected by the sight of a bombed bridge. They cram along the sides, peering down into the craters and holes, looking very sad and crying."[6]

People increasingly poured into Al-Radi's orchard as their houses were hit. But the noise was so deafening that some in her group even wanted to sign up for the shelters. When Al-Radi finally went to the shelter closest to her orchard, she was told to sign in by six o'clock as per curfew, and that she would only be let out the next morning. Although the conditions were cramped, with no toilet facilities and even no windows, she convinced her ever-growing group to stay despite the hardship, feeling so exposed as the bombs and rockets landed all around them. And then came "[a] turning point in the war. They hit a shelter, the one in Amiriya. They thought it was going to be full of party biggies but instead it turned out to be full of women and children. Whole families were wiped out. Only some of the men survived who had remained to guard their houses. An utter horror and we don't know the worst of it yet. The Americans insist that the women and children were put there on purpose. I ask you, is that logical? One can imagine the conversation at command headquarters going something like this: 'Well, I think the Americans will hit the Amirya shelter next. Let's fill it with women and children.' What makes the Americans think they are invincible? In their very short history they've had more than their share of blunders and mistakes. Imagine my going to check up on our shelter two days before they bombed the Amiriya. Who would want to use the shelters anymore? My neighbors say they now prefer to live with the noise."[7]

As the bombing continued day in and day out, "what makes life livable" indeed completely disintegrated. The bombings in 1991 were not "shock and awe." The pathos of the weakness of the Iraqi missile defense is summarized in Al-Radi's sorrowful and yet ironic statement on day 31: "[t]he score today is 76,000 Allied air raids versus 67 Scuds."[8] Al-Radi repeats the oft-quoted estimate that the United States ultimately dropped five times the firepower of Hiroshima on Baghdad. The Iraqi defenses could do nothing to protect against such an onslaught. Indeed, the launching capacity for the scuds was clearly poor. The Al-Radis, in fact, had their closest call when a scud launched from one part of Baghdad blew up over their house and orchard. "It must have been about 9 p.m. and we were all in the kitchen washing up in the flickering candlelight after dinner. . . . Suddenly there was a terrible noise and a bright light coming closer and closer, a sun homing into us through the kitchen windows, a white, unreal daylight illuminating us all. The floor was shaking so violently that we thought the house was coming down on our heads. We crouched on the floor, and suddenly without our knowing how, the door opened and all six of us were outside in the garden. An immense fireball was hovering over us, a fireball that appeared to be burning the tops of the palm trees. Suddenly this giant flaming object tilted, turned upwards over our heads and went roaring up into the night sky. . . . We discovered later from the BBC that it was a Scud missile, launched from a mobile truck. It landed in Bahrain. At the time we couldn't decide whether it was a plane, a missile or a rocket, or even whether it was coming or going. For the first time since the war began, I thought it was all over for us. I'm sure that if its trajectory had been a few metres different we would have been incinerated. It was like watching a rocket launch from Cape Canaveral except this was no television and we were underneath the blast."[9] On the 40th day, Al-Radi describes her exhaustion and her sadness. "Nights and days full of noise, no sleep possible. What will happen to all of us now? For forty odd days and nights—a biblical figure—we've just been standing around with our mouths open, swallowing bombs, figuratively speaking, that is. We didn't have anything to do with the Kuwaiti take-over, yet we have been paying the price for it . . . We're living in an Indian movie, or rather like Peter Sellers in *The Party*, refusing to die and rising up again and again, another last gasp on the bugle. In comparison, we come up every now and then with a Scud. Indian movies never really end, and I don't think this scenario will end either. If it were not such a tragedy, it would be quite funny."[10]

With this account, am I simply trying to prod the imagination so that we can envision what it might be like to live under "shock and awe" as a much more intense bombardment than the one Al-Radi endured? Am I instead trying to help us to come to terms with why "they" might hate us other than the oft-repeated phrase "they hate us for our way of life"? It is actually a combination of both, with an emphasis ultimately on why we, as citizens of the United States, must confront what has been done in our name and in the name of the just war tradition, which I will discuss more in a moment. For we do need to hear Al-Radi, as she struggles with the visceral reaction she has to Westerners. Al-Radi was trained in the West and as an internationally proclaimed artist, she has traveled all over the world. Although she was raised as a Muslim, she is not a follower of Islam. As an artist, democracy and free expression are crucial to her. As an unmarried independent woman, she has never accepted any conventional feminine restrictions, imposed by the Muslim religion or otherwise, on her life. During her years in Iraq where she grew up, none were enforced by the state. Sometimes we forget that for all of Hussein's brutality toward his enemies, women participated in all professions in Iraq. Those who wore any kind of veil did so only by choice.

On the 33rd day of the war, Al-Radi sees a Westerner for the first time and fights back her reaction to him. "Hisham came this morning to pay his condolences on Mundher's death and to say hello. He has been in Suleimaniya all this time; apparently a lot of people went there to get away from the bombing. He was followed by Tim Llewellyn, the first foreigner I have seen since the war began. I have cousins who are married to Brits but they have been here so long they are tainted. One does not think of them anymore as foreign. When I saw Tim at the bottom of the drive, I literally bristled. I wonder if he felt it? I'm happy to say that by the time he had come up our long drive I had gotten over my hostile feelings. After all, one cannot blame individuals for what their governments do. Otherwise we would all have to answer for the mess we're in, and we surely had no hand in this matter. Tim brought faxes from Sol, Dood, and Charlie, our first contact with family and friends. A break in our isolation."[11]

The question "why do they hate us?" has been frequently asked since 9/11. But within the question, the "they" has been hopelessly vague. Does it refer to the highly educated Saudi men who drove the planes into the World Trade Center? Does it refer to Bin Laden and Al-Qaeda? Does it refer to the Iraqis? Does the question presume the existence of something called the Arab world, which lumps together many different peoples, languages, and traditions, that hates us? Or is the question only why do the followers of one particularly conservative and militant brand of Islam, Wahhabism, hate us. Wahhabism is the sect of Islam that dominates Saudi Arabia, but were the hijackers of the planes on 9/11 Wahhabis? We do not know that for sure because they left no notes or messages behind. But when we ask why "they" hate us, we need to be careful as to whom we are speaking of in the Arab world so that we can at least begin to discuss whether any of that bitterness and rage is warranted and, if so, what are we, as U.S. citizens, called to do about it. I am not speaking of Bin Laden himself, for he clearly calls for the execution of U.S. citizens and the citizens of other Western governments who support U.S. foreign policy wherever and whenever they can be targeted. He is undoubtedly a criminal with whom negotiations are impossible. We know why he hates "us," saying over and over again that "we" are "infidels." But I am more interested in beginning to make distinctions in that huge amorphous "they," for Al-Radi's embattled rage has absolutely nothing to do with Bin Laden. It is time that we in the United States begin to see the distinctiveness of cultures and peoples, and divergent interpretations of the Muslim religion in that utterly amorphous "they" that George W. Bush many times evokes. Al-Radi's rage clearly did not come from any jealousy or distaste for modernity and democracy. However, her bitterness toward the senior Bush administration remained. "Well, Mr. Bush said no to the overtures of Tariq Aziz. I never thought he would say yes anyway. It doesn't serve his purpose. What a brave man, he passes judgment on us while he plays golf far away in Washington. His forces are annihilating us . . . I can't stand the Voice of America going on about American children and how they are being affected by this war. Mrs. Bush, the so-called humane member of that marriage, had the gall to say comfortingly to a group of school kids, 'Don't worry, it's far away and won't affect you.' What about the children here? What double standards, what hypocrisy! Where is justice?"[12]

Her question is addressed to all of us who are citizens of this country. Although I will later point out the limits of just war theory, we still need to remember that at the heart of the just war tradition is the demand that the aggressors—citizens of the aggressor state included—take responsibility and accept that they can be held accountable to those upon whom they have waged war. Jean Bethke Elshtain summarizes the notion of the citizen in just war theory as follows: "Just war thinking as a form of civic virtue cannot endorse the unleashing of aggressivity sanctioned by armed civic virtue in a time of total war. Indeed, what is demanded instead is deep reflection by Everyman and Everywoman on what his or her government is up to. This, in turn, presupposes a "self" of a certain kind, one attuned to moral reasoning and capable of it; one strong enough to resist the lure of seductive, violent enthusiasms; one bounded by and laced through with a sense of responsibility and accountability."[13]

Whatever one thinks about the Gulf War, it was frequently justified with the rhetoric and under the rubric of just war theory. Al-Radi's challenges us to think about how we can live with the hypocrisy and the double standard in which Iraqi lives are not accorded the same dignity and status we give to our own. To give such status to one's enemies may indeed be seen as the heart or core of the long process of the legalization of war that ultimately culminates in just war theory. So all those who take just war seriously have to at least confront the seriousness of the charge that the double standard provokes great hostility in those who are subjected to it, as it would provoke in ourselves if we felt we were not accorded dignity.

Richard Falk has succinctly defined the four principles of just war theory as follows:

Discrimination: any use of force should discriminate between military and civilian targets, and unconditionally avoid targeting the latter regardless of military necessity; civilian innocence should be respected without exception in the course of the waging war.
Proportionality: any use of force should have some reasonable relationship between the responsibility, resistance, and capabilities of the target state and the level and intensity and goals of response by the state acting in self-defense.
Necessity: any use of force should be essential to the attainment of legitimate military objectives; excessive force should be avoided.
Humanity: any use of force should uphold international humanitarian law, and avoid any human suffering not reasonably related to necessary and reasonable military objectives.[14]

These four principles all turn on both the accordance of the status of human being to citizens of the enemy state, and to ourselves as those who must judge the actions of our government. I do not think the bombing of Baghdad in the first Gulf War was just under just war standards. But at least then the rhetoric if not the practice of just war was still alive and well, even in the administration of Bush Senior. Of course, just war theory can be manipulated and should ultimately be replaced by the ideal of perpetual peace with its correspondingly much more limited notion of what can be legitimate counter-violence. But that is not my point here, although I will return to it shortly. As Jean Elshtain points out, just war theory not only applies to war and its means in armed conflict, but also allows us to question other means of fighting a people once the armed conflict has actually ended. For example, just war theory looks at how peace is established because the enemy, even if vanquished, is still part of humanity. For Elshtain, just war theory demanded that we carefully examine the embargo and sanctions that we imposed on the Iraqi people. As Elshtain eloquently wrote, "[m]y interest in the Gulf War and just war revolved, not so much around whether the central criteria for involvement were or were not met, but with what just war thinking more widely understood might tell us about politics in general as well as about one war in particular. My concern wasn't that just war thinking shouldn't be hauled out on various rhetorical or ceremonial occasions and then shelved once the political moment has passed. I argued that if just war is evoked, then that is the framework that must be applied consistently, not just to the strategy of war fighting but to the endgame as well—to how one handles the post war situation. As of this writing, Iraqi citizens are suffering greatly under a continuing set of economic sanctions that appear to have little effect on Saddam Hussein's ability to hold on to power. Just war thinking would suggest that this form of (apparent) benign intervention, by contrast to actual war fighting, is not in fact ethically pristine, even apart from whether or not it is politically effective. The rush to use embargoes and sanctions that target whole populations, harming the least powerful first, requires more justification than it has received from past and current policy makers."[15]

I am in complete agreement with Elshtain in her epilogue to *Women and War*. Yes, we must look at the end game of "peace" once the hostilities of actual combat have ceased. And we again, as citizens of the United States, are called to such scrutiny by just war theory. Yet in her latest book, Elshtain attacks Edward Said for exaggerating the effects of the embargo. Elshtain challenges the figure used by Said and many others— including for example the Dominican Order of Nuns, which continues at this writing to be in Iraq—that 500,000 children have died because of improper food and medical care. Usually when that figure is cited, deaths from illnesses caused by uranium shells and other side effects of the bombs dropped during the Gulf War on Iraq are included.[16] Of course, the exact number of casualties is difficult to estimate. But interestingly, when Madeline Albright was confronted with this figure on CNN in 1996 when she was still the U.S. ambassador to the UN, she did not deny it. Instead, she remarked that it "was a hard choice" but that ultimately the "price was worth it."[17] Indeed, Albright, rather than denying the figure, seemed to want to confirm it because it showed how bad life was going to continue to be under Saddam Hussein. That was a bad mistake on her part if indeed the figure is so obviously exaggerated as Elshtain contends. Does her statement represent the kind of double standard and hypocrisy that Al-Radi demands we face? It certainly does under just war theory because, as Elshtain points out, it is the most powerless in society who are targeted by this kind of embargo, particularly under a corrupt regime. Al-Radi gives us a description of the hospitals in Baghdad under the embargo. "Maysa, Suhair's daughter, said there's too much talk these days about Gulf War Syndrome. Everyone has that, it's the norm now in Baghdad. But we're dealing with basic diseases like cholera, polio, TB, major stuff, she continued. Gulf War Syndrome talk is for those who don't know what's happening in the hospitals. Gynaecologists are reusing disposable gloves, just dipping them in Dettol, same with disposable syringes. The anesthetic that is used has come as gifts from various countries, different brands, and no one knows the strengths or what dosage to give to patients—one woman took fifteen hours to wake up from an anesthetic injection after a Caesarean operation. Surgical thread is some old-fashioned stuff from Pakistan that takes five to eight months to dissolve and causes infections and complications. Anyone over fifty years old is told that there are no medicines; doctors want to keep what little there is for younger patients. That's the level we've reached."[18]

But Elshtain's point is that we—U.S. citizens—should not blame the United States because both food and medicine were supposed to be allowed into the country. Furthermore, the UN, at least initially, authorized the embargo. According to Elshtain, Saddam Hussein is also responsible because he was supposedly misusing the allocations. I do not doubt that Hussein was incredibly corrupt. As Al-Radi bitterly remarks, "[e]veryone seems to be dying of cancer. Every day one hears about another acquaintance or friend of a friend dying. How many more die in hospitals that one does not know? Apparently over thirty percent of Iraqis have cancer, and there are lots of kids with leukaemia. They will never lift the embargo off us. Saddam appeared on TV this evening, stating that Albright's speech was a pack of lies. Nothing is in my name, he said, it's all for the state. True enough, he doesn't need to put anything in his name. The whole country is his."[19]

Was not Elshtain's point in her earlier work that it is precisely because of such corruption that the embargo would not have its intended effect of weakening the Hussein regime? Did we expect him to fairly partition out the UN rations? Does Elshtain believe for one minute that if the United States had gone to the UN and asked for the lifting of the embargo, that it would not have been lifted? I doubt that she does or did. Hussein's corruption does not get us—U.S. citizens—off the hook; at least it cannot under the understanding of just war theory that Elshtain advocates. Of course, Elshtain is attacking Said for another purpose. She is accusing him, as a representative of the left in the academy, of trying to say that somehow we deserved 9/11 because of things like the embargo in Iraq. I do not believe Said ever said or meant that. But the point that should be made is subtler, and one that Elshtain should find herself sympathetic to, given her own emphasis on the importance of civic virtue. We have to take responsibility for the justness of our actions, regardless of what anyone else does to us. No matter how bad 9/11 was, it should not be a reason for rejecting what is best in just war theory and the responsibility it places on us to examine our past and, indeed, to help us examine more carefully why "they" hate us. Just war theory always calls for this kind of examination and care.

Particularly in these very troubled times, we need to remind ourselves of that more than ever. The embargo was wrong under just war theory for all the reasons that Elshtain suggests. Wrong actions that cause harm breed hostility. To recognize that point is completely different than to suggest that past actions of the United States justified the deaths of 3000 people in the World Trade Center. That is a ridiculous claim, and one that I agree with Elshtain, as well as Said, about. Just war theory calls us to examine our past so as to guide us in our future. The events of 9/11 make that examination, which is exactly what many peace activists and critics of the Bush administration have insisted upon, even more urgent. But such examination will only be accepted if the Bush administration were still operating under a just war rubric and rhetoric, which it obviously is not.

"Shock and Awe" flagrantly broke with the just war framework, and the remnants of the theory are hardly encouraging. The New York Times reported that Rumsfeld told the commanders in the field to ask for his permission if they planned military actions that would involve killing more than 30 civilians. Five hundred such raids were requested and all were given the green light, which raises serious doubts as to whether Rumsfeld actually scrutinized any of the requests. As the days and months pass and the war in Iraq continues, which was recently called guerilla war for the first time, we certainly see great hatred directed at the United States. Unfortunately, it is the young men and women in the field who are bearing the brunt of that hatred. What does it mean to give up the rhetoric and rubric of just war, as I accuse the Bush administration of doing in the war on Iraq? It means that there is no longer even the pretense that those on the other side, the citizens of Iraq, are accorded the status of human beings. The rhetoric of *The New York Post* should horrify us all. The gleeful contempt—not only over the bombing of a magnificent city and its people, but also over the tragic destruction of the cradle of civilization—that is grotesque indeed. As the novelist and essayist Arundhati Roy angrily wrote shortly after the bombing started, "Mesopotamia. Babylon. The Tigris and Euphrates. How many children, in how many classrooms have hang-glided through the past transported on the wings of these words? And now the bombs are falling, incinerating and humiliating that ancient civilization."[20] When Bush, as reported by CNN, gave the final order to begin the bombing early, due to the intelligence that Hussein and his son were together and potentially easy targets, he purportedly waved his fist and announced it to "feel good."

As Elshtain writes in her latest book, "[i]n the aftermath of a conflict in which force has been deployed, politics is more likely to flourish if the temptations of religious triumphalism and nationalistic chauvinism have been avoided during the conflict."[21] Indeed, it should never "feel good" to go to war; and if it does, then it certainly implicates George W. Bush in worrisome national chauvinism. Here, we are extremely far from the sober rhetoric of just war theory, which always takes war to be a last resort. But of course, this war was not a last resort. The UN inspectors were still continuing to look for weapons of mass destruction when ordered out of Iraq. As it became clear that the United States would not gain a majority in the Security Council, it announced its intention to invade Iraq alone, at that time still justifying it as self-defense against weapons of mass destruction and Hussein's purported connection with Al-Qaeda—a strange accusation indeed because the Sunnis and the Wahhabis have a long history of bitter contest within Islam.[22] Since then, it has increasingly become evident that there were no weapons of mass destruction because none were found and none were used. Indeed, there was no sale of uranium from Niger to Saddam Hussein—a piece of evidence Bush heavily relied upon in his insistence that Iraq had weapons of mass destruction. More poignantly, we have Al-Radi's description of the pathetic state of the Iraqi air defense system during the Gulf War where scuds were launched from mobile trucks to blow up above the heads of their own people. Were we to believe that a country subject to the embargo and to constant surveillance could find the means to build such weapons? We had once supplied Hussein with weaponry but were clearly no longer doing so, and nor was the Soviet Union, no longer existing as such.[23] Although it was an implausible claim to begin with, only after the war had already begun was it declared a humanitarian invasion to free the Iraqi people. Yet the change in justification did not change the means of the war. Is freedom to be won through shock and awe? And of course, as a matter of international law, humanitarian invasions must proceed through the UN. The war against Iraq was illegal and unjust and all of us, the Iraqis, the soldiers in the field, and those bearing the financial cost of the war, are now suffering the consequences. I do think we owe money and economic support to the Iraqi people because we have unnecessarily wreaked havoc on their country, and would call this money reparations. After what we have done, we cannot simply leave the country. But it is a heavy price to demand of U.S. citizens for a war that we should not have fought. If it is too late to prevent the war in Iraq, it is not too late to demand a return to respect for international law, and what could and should amount to a just humanitarian action. We need to understand how the war against Iraq was allowed to take place with a sliding set of justifications. The peace movement certainly attempted such a critique. On February 15, 2003, one bitterly cold day in New York City, hundreds of thousands of people took to the streets, joined by thousands of others in demonstrations throughout the country and millions upon millions of others throughout the world. The sheer numbers should make this day stand out in history and should continue to give hope to those who have not forsaken the ideal of perpetual peace.

Of course, I think that a return to the rubric of the legality of war would also be a step forward. But even that is not enough for the process of reconciliation that must go on in the UN, within international law, and if I can sound grandiose, with many of the peoples of the world who have been threatened by the United States and frightened by its lawlessness. I am certain that it is scary to be threatened by the power of the United States. It is even scarier now to be threatened by the United States when it has shown its willingness to discard international law, ignore the United Nations, and unilaterally turn its military might against a nation-state. As citizens of the United States, we must insist that our government obey international law. We must do it in the streets in the best of the U.S. tradition as we did on February 15th, March 21st, and April 29th, 2003. We must also continue to defend what is best in the constitutional tradition of the United States.

I am with Lawrence Lapham when he writes, "[w]hat joins the Americans one to another is not a common nationality, race, or ancestry, but their voluntary pledge to a shared work of both the moral and political imagination. My love of country follows from a love of its freedom, not from pride in its armies and fleets, and I admire the institutions of American government as useful and well-made tools (on the order of plow, an axe, or a surveyor's plumb line) meant to support the liberties of the people, not the ambitions of the state. The Constitution serves as the premise for a narrative rather than as a design for a monument or as a plan for invasion."[24]

This explains those of us who were distressed by Bush ending the "battle" with Iraq on the deck of the aircraft carrier. What lies at the heart of the constitutional narrative is that the executive branch is limited and does not rule by exception. Thoughtful critics like Ronald Dworkin raised serious issues about the USA PATRIOT Act's effects on the Bill of Rights and, in a second article, challenged the constitutionality of military tribunals.[25] I will not repeat those arguments here. I wish to focus for now on Section 2 Public Law 107-40 (S.J. Resolution 23), which gave President Bush the authority to act against "any future acts of international terrorism against the United States by such nations, organizations, or persons."[26] Jean Elshtain argues that the critics of the President wrongly accused the administration for declaring the war on Afghanistan. Under the bill, the President was given powers to declare such a war and he undoubtedly did so. The concern voiced by one brave Congresswoman was that it was a mistake to give the President of the United States these kinds of powers, even after the crisis of 9/11. Elshtain argues that several times in history, the staunch insistence that it is Congress and Congress alone in which the war-making powers abide has been put aside, including in the Civil War. There have been such exceptions and none worried about them harder or more eloquently than did Lincoln during the Civil War. Lincoln took extraordinary measures as he told the people, because the Constitution and the fate of the nation were at stake. Lincoln was right to worry because the spirit of the Constitution goes against the grain of extending special war-making powers. Elshtain, in the statement she helped to pen, "What are we fighting for?," signs on to the proposition that one of our most basic values is "the conviction that because our individual and collective access to truth is imperfect, most disagreements about values call for civility, openness to other views, and reasonable argument in pursuit of truth."[27] New York State Senator Hillary Clinton simplistically explained, "You are either for us or against us." This rhetoric might be appropriate for football games but it is not appropriate for serious political crises such as the one brought on by 9/11. Many of us in the peace movement worried about many of the provisions in the USA PATRIOT Act, and were concerned that our country not be frightened into rejecting its fundamental liberal and constitutional values.

I am more than aware that there are many different kinds of liberalisms, particularly philosophical liberalisms. Here, I am using liberalism as a stand-in for the idea fundamental to U.S. constitutionalism, that sovereignty is limited and balanced by the three branches of state power so that too much power is never put in the hands of the executive branch. This is liberalism understood as a form of governmentality, and it is this liberalism that I endorse and that I worry has been seriously weakened in our public discourse and in provisions of the USA PATRIOT Act such as Section 2, as a matter of law. I believe it is important to declare oneself liberal in this sense because it is so fundamental to both our constitutional schema and to the promotion of the civility that inheres in the idea that no one has or should have the last word on truth in politics. Here I agree with Elshtain. But when she writes, "[w]hen Hannah Arendt was asked whether she was a liberal or a conservative, she criticized the question. 'No real illumination ever comes out of thinking in ideological categories,' she noted, 'for that is not thinking at all. Categorical rigidities, inhibit thought rather than promote reflection.' Michael Walzer has been led to call the (academic) leftist critique of U.S. foreign policy, with its blanket condemnation, 'stupid overwrought, grossly inaccurate'."[28] I am not sure how we get from Arendt to Walzer on foreign policy, so let me stick to my central point in this essay; that point is to respond to Walzer's criticism of the peace movement.

Sometimes in politics we need to configure, justify, and defend ideals. Ideological categories, at least within one definition, are broadly drawn configurations of ideals. Socialism is a perfect example of an ideal of radical change in the organization of the economy and the democratic organization of the state. The "end of ideology," particularly when it defends political realisms, is often a mask for the critique of idealism in all forms. Certainly there are dangers in defending ideals; we need to worry about self-righteous moralizing that ends rather than promotes democratic debate. But we must insist on the necessity of reclaiming and defending ideals. I am with the philosopher Étienne Balibar when he writes, "that there is no liberation from violence, no resistance to its worst excesses, especially no collective resistance (but a resistance that is not collective can hardly be called a resistance) without ideals.[29] So liberalism as I have defined it as a form of governmentality embodies an ideal of the rule of law that rests on basic liberties and limits of sovereignty. If Elshtain and Walzer remain liberals in this sense, I would ask that they clearly state so.

In the fall of 2002, Ann Snitow and myself organized a group that would defend this sense of liberalism, among other ideals. That group became known as Take Back the Future. What worried us both then and now is that "us versus them" rhetoric encourages the undermining of our Constitution and Bill of Rights. Hence, our agenda was to actively remember the Bill of Rights with our feet. We marched without a permit in front of Penn Station while some recited the Bill of Rights and others chased those reciting under the cover of a giant 15-foot worm. We marched without a permit, while respecting New York City ordinances, to remind people about why the Bill of Rights is so important and why we were worried about the USA PATRIOT Act. I like to think of our strategies in this and other actions last fall and spring as meeting another one of Elshtain's ideals—this one about political action itself. She writes, "[t]he dream I am dreaming as I end these reflections is not one of solemn deed doers but of zestful act takers, experimenting with new possibilities playfully but from a deep seriousness of purpose."[30]

But to understand the seriousness of purpose behind our efforts on behalf of the Bill of Rights, we need to contrast the position I believe we stood for against that of the famous anti-liberal Carl Schmitt. The German philosopher and journalist Carolin Emcke succinctly summarizes Schmitt's concept of politics and forcefully argues that it is Schmitt's notion of politics that is closest to explaining the Bush administration's public rhetoric. "'Sovereign is he who decides the exception,' Carl Schmitt states, and the war on terrorism justifies its extra-legal actions, its disruptions of former conventions or norms of legitimacy, its transgression of laws and human or civil rights by declaring a state of emergency. Parallel, Schmitt introduces a concept of the political which situates the friend–enemy distinction as its prime objective. The friend–enemy distinction is the matrix along which politics creates its own purpose. 'The high points of politics are simultaneously the moments in which the enemy is, in concrete clarity, recognized as the enemy.' In this respect, the friend–enemy distinction and politics constitute one another. The enemy in its almost ontological difference is perceived as a threat to the general order, and insofar always functions as an occasion for a reenactment of sovereign power. The concept of the political, for Schmitt, almost depends on the enemy, because only in recognizing the enemy as an enemy does politics appear. And only when responding to the threat that the enemy poses, can politics stage and present itself as sovereign power—able to suspend law. The paradoxical Schmittian logic of self-protection suggests that when the order is under attack, the order can be lifted. When the norms are under threat, the norms can be transgressed."[31]

It is this dangerous paradox that has been of concern to many people on the left who have criticized aspects of the USA PATRIOT Act. There is also the worry that the need to designate the enemy was leading to the targeting of innocent Muslims. In her statement "What are we fighting for?," Elshtain and the other signatories write that, "[w]e wish especially to reach out to our brothers and sisters in Muslim societies. We say to you forthrightly: we are not enemies, but friends. We must not be enemies. We have so much in common. There is so much we must do together. Your human dignity, no less than ours—your rights and opportunities for a good life, no less than ours—are what we believe we are fighting for. We know that, for some of you, mistrust of us is high, and we know that we Americans are partly responsible for that mistrust. But we must not be enemies. In hope, we wish to join with you and all people of good will to build a just and lasting peace."[32]

Yet despite this proclamation, Elshtain frequently falls into pessimism about dialogue with the Muslim religion, assuming that the Wahhabism faction has won the day. Elshtain mistakenly writes that Islamic fundamentalism is a product of the 20th century. Wahhbism has generated opposition within the Islamic world since its founding. There is a long history that Muslims can and do rely on in their battle against this particular faction within the Muslim religion. Part of the rich and varied tradition in Islam is the struggle against certain interpretations and social prescriptions of the Wahhab sect. The history of the battle against Wahhabism, which began in the 17th century, is as long as Wahhabism itself. As Tariq Ali writes, "[o]n their own, Ibn Wahhab's views would have been harmless. It was his social prescriptions—a belief in Islamic punishment beatings, an insistence on the stoning death of adulterers, the amputation of thieves and public execution of criminals—that created real problems in 1740. Religious leaders in the region objected strongly when he began to practice what he preached. Annoyed by this nonsense and fearing a popular revolt, the emir of Uyayna asked the preacher to leave the city."[33] Simply put, Wahhabism has always met with resistance in the Islamic world. Part of the disagreement within the religion in the 18th century was the conflation of crime as sin. Elshtain seems to believe that this conflation is true of all conservative groups within the Muslim religion, without giving us any definition of what conservative means in the context of the Muslim religion. Of course, she is right that Wahhabism has, in fact, enjoyed increasing popularity in the 20th century. The social prescriptions of the Taliban were the result of the leaders' identification with Wahhabism. Bin Laden identifies with Wahhabism. And Wahhabism is the state religion of his home country, Saudi Arabia. Indeed, it is also Wahhabism that promotes Bin Laden's brand of *jihad*. Elshtain writes about the terrible situation of women under the Taliban, which tragically continues under the Northern Alliance. Many of the warlords of the Alliance also identify with Wahhabism, which is why the Revolutionary Association of Women in Afghanistan was so aghast that some feminists in the United States could possibly support the Northern Alliance as a coalition of hope. That feminists could do so was, in part, the result of their ignorance of the Muslim religion and the Arab world. Admittedly, I know very little about the Muslim religion myself, although I have sought to educate myself. Still recognizing how little I know, it seems crucial that we follow the advice of those within Islam who do have this knowledge. Thus, for example, U.S. feminists should do everything they can to support groups like RAWA that have tirelessly fought for the rights of women in Afghanistan. Muslim women within RAWA fight for women's rights from within interpretations of the sacred texts. For more than 20 years, RAWA has sought to bring the plight of the Afghan people to the world, hoping against hope for international support. Elshtain writes at length about the horrific situation of the women of Afghanistan and other Muslim countries. I encourage her to give support to the feminist organizations within those countries that are working tirelessly to change the situation. One way we can help to build the kind of trust that Elshtain call us to, is by supporting these organizations rather than making it seem as if Muslim women simply accept their fate and victimization. This also helps to fight against the stereotypes of Muslim women. "It is unfair," Elshtain writes, "to moderate Muslims and to the brave Muslim women fighting for democratic reform to refuse to criticize radical Islamicism's severe gender practices by burying them under the label 'cultural diversity.' Such 'tolerance' is wrongheaded at best. It is not diversity we are talking about but systematic, legally mandated cruelty that goes so far as to threaten the lives of women and even to destroy their lives capriciously should they violate a draconian directive about the consequences of sinful behavior."[34] I think that RAWA would agree with Elshtain here, as along as she accepts that feminism is neither Western nor incompatible with the Muslim religion per se. At times, however, Elshtain comes close to attributing her pessimism about the dialogues she promotes with the Muslim religion to the situation of women in Muslim countries. There have always been powerful feminist movements in these countries. During this century there have also been periods in many Arab countries where significant reforms have been won. Women played major roles in all walks of life under Hussein's rule in Iraq. It is far from a monolithic picture or story. Here again, she must be careful to separate out Wahhabism from other strands of a very rich and varied tradition.

Ultimately however, her pessimism seems to come from her conviction that there are too many irrational Wahhabites in today's Muslim circles, even in the United States.

She holds "[t]oo many imams in Western Europe as well as in Muslim countries 'preach murderous hatred of the United States' including the admonition that 'Christian and Jews should have their throats slit' according to an article in *The New York Times*. Sadly, wild conspiracy theories are also current in much discourse promulgated by extremists but picked up and apparently given wide currency in the Arab streets."[35]

I cannot speak directly to what is being picked up on Arab streets. My suspicion is that Elshtain is in no better position to know either, which is why I would caution her about drawing too many conclusions about what is to her "apparently" so. But when she writes about the Islamic Circle of North America, I do have something to say. Elshtain writes,

There are strains of self-criticism in the wind, including the fact Sheik Muhammad Hisham Kabbani, a prominent Sufi cleric living in America, just two short years ago issued a "chilling admonition to Americans to beware the Muslims in their midst," a warning that was widely regarded as overwrought. 'Sheik Kabbani said that American Muslim groups were dominated by Sufi-hating Wahhabis, and when he tried to distribute pamphlets at the annual conference of the Islamic Society of North America, organizers called the police. For his troubles, Sheik Kabbani received FBI protection because of threats against his life.[36]

We do not get any more information of how the Sheik might have behaved at that meeting which would promote that reaction. I would need to know more about that particular incident before I could make a judgment about it. The Islamic Circle of North America is an umbrella organization that works to protect the interests of all Muslims within North America. It promises non-sectarianism, peaceful debate, and education. In December of 2002, I had several meetings with the Islamic Circle of North America, where I met Sufis, Sunnites, and Shi'as, all of whom were working together. I never met a Wahhabi. The different groups clearly worked well and effectively together in their tireless efforts on behalf of the Muslim community. Take Back the Future was welcomed and our efforts to support them were deeply appreciated. I asked many questions and found the dialogue that Elshtain calls for more than possible. We sought to work with the Islamic Circle in opposing the practice of registering legal male residents from Arab countries, which targeted them for religious beliefs and identifications. Our main concern was religious freedom, an ideal that we share with Elshtain. We were asked by the Islamic Circle of North America to participate in a series of demonstrations in front of the INS in New York City, and were there with the "worm" as requested. The police allowed us out of the barricade and we circulated with our performance, reciting the First Amendment as we walked around the blocks close to the INS. Many were sympathetic to what we had to say, but we also encountered virulent anti-Muslim sentiment. A number of us had witnessed the targeting of innocent men and women in the Muslim community, and we wanted to show that not all citizens of the United States felt that way. Trust has to be built. Elshtain downplays the problem of targeting Muslims after 9/11. She writes, "[i]n an essay in Egypt's *Al-Ahram Weekly*, the celebrated American academic Edward Said does precisely this, beginning with the claim that Arabs and Muslims in the United States now face 'targeted hostility.' He speaks of 'many reported instances of discriminatory behavior against Arabs,' who draw 'unwelcome attention' if they speak Arabic. He claims that Arabs are 'usually made to stand aside for special attention during airport security checks.' (I fly at least twice a week, usually more often, and I have never seen this happen; indeed, the directives sent down by the

Secretary of Transportation prohibiting ethnic and racial profiling make it less likely that persons of Arab descent will be singled out. This is not to say that it never happens, but it is not official policy."[37]

The registration of men from Muslim countries was indeed official policy, and I would certainly call it "targeted hostility" as well as a serious denial of the respect we should give to every religion. We must learn to appreciate the diversity and richness within the Arab world itself. It is crucial for the peace movement to fight against the stereotypes. There are Muslims who are struggling to address "the crisis" in Islam as Elshtain calls it. In a moment of beauty and grace in his letter to a young Muslim, Tariq Ali writes, "[h]ere you discover that as long as Islamist governments open their countries to global penetration, they will be permitted to do what they want in the socio-political realm. The American Empire used Islam and it can do it again. Here lies the challenge. We are in desperate need of an Islamic Reformation that sweeps away the crazed conservatism and backwardness of the fundamentalists, but, more than that, opens the world of Islam to new ideas which are seen to be more advanced than what is currently on offer from the West. This would necessitate a rigid separation of state and mosque; the dissolution of the clergy; the assertion by Muslim intellectuals of their right to interpret the texts that are the collective property of Islamic culture as a whole; the freedom to think freely and rationally and the freedom of the imagination. Unless we move in this direction we will be doomed to re-living old battles, and thinking not of a richer and humane future, but of how we can move from the present to the past. It is an unacceptable vision."[38]

I have no doubt that the "war on terror," as well as the stereotypes about the moral indifference to the suffering we impose, has enhanced both fear of and hatred toward the United States. Even our continuing efforts to track Al-Qaeda in Afghanistan are impeded by fear of the United States and its armed forces. We still have a long way to go in this effort.

As a story in the *New York Times Magazine* reports, "according to terrorism experts at the International Institute for Strategic Studies, a London-based policy group devoted largely to world security, the estimates run something like this: about 20,000 jihadic soldiers had graduated from Al Qaeda's training camps in Afghanistan as of October 2001, when the American-led war began there. Up to 10,000 of those were in Afghanistan at the time. Since then, the coalition campaign has killed or captured around 2000. Ninety percent of Bin Laden's forces, and more than half of his commanders, remain free. And no one is quite sure where they are. Some of the Arabs among them have probably made their way back to the Middle East. Many of the rest seem to straddle the frontiers of Afghanistan, Pakistan, and neighboring Iran. Al Qaeda is, the institute judges, 'more insidious and just as dangerous' as before the 9/11 attacks."[39]

Those of us who favored a police action against Al-Qaeda did so in part because many of us felt that it was the only effective way to address 9/11. But we had to gain support from within the Arab world for our actions. The war in Iraq leaves us more discredited than ever.

My real disagreement with Elshtain, then, is both practical and a matter of principle. The United States simply cannot and should not be the main proponent of humanitarian values in the world. As Richard Falk eloquently and succinctly writes, "I believe the Bush administration has been doing its best to wreck world order as it had been evolving, and that part of the wreckage is the abandonment of legal restraints on the use of international force, the heart and soul of the UN charter. The Iraq war epitomized this process. The world needs the international will and capabilities to rescue vulnerable populations from impending humanitarian catastrophes, but it doesn't need imperial wars that hide their true character in the fog of moralizing rhetoric."[40]

The disagreement in principle with Elshtain is that the just war rubric, although it is certainly better than the lawlessness of the Bush administration, is not adequate to achieve the goals Falk seeks. Instead, we need to affirm the ideal of peace. Elshtain often mocks peace, as if it were an absolute end to violence. But she misunderstands what is meant by an ideal here. An ideal is not a goal, but a horizon of the future that guides us in how violence is defined. As the philosopher Étienne Balibar has written, in a sense violence is redefined as preventive counter-violence, one example of which could be humanitarian intervention. Those who favor the ideal of peace in the place of just war rhetoric do so, in part, because just war rubric is completely caught up in the nation-state as the highest form of political community. Indeed, Elshtain herself warns against the danger of a crusading nationalism that lingers in just war theory. She writes, "[h]ow to explain popular savagery? In part it stems from the crusading impulse lurking in the interstices of just war theory. The language of good and evil, just and unjust, may under conditions that invite total war turn people out as judges who sometimes become executioners."[41]

If we are to achieve a world in which preventive counter-violence can be judged as necessary and fair, we clearly need transnational institutions that no longer place the nation-state as the only or even the main deployer of preventive counter-violence. This does not mean that I think that the nation-state will simply disappear, or that RAWA is wrong to fight for a free, independent, and democratic Afghanistan. It is to say that the place of the nation-state will lose its unquestioned centrality in world politics that promote the ideal of perpetual peace. After the war in Iraq has so badly hurt the United Nations and other transnational institutions, the peace movement has much work to do. Our efforts have never been more necessary in the face of this "wreckage" Falk so eloquently describes.

Worlds Apart: Perpetual Peace and Infinite War   2

I was opposed to the war in Afghanistan for both ethical and strategic reasons. In the forums and teach-ins in which I participated after the terrorist acts, I wanted more than anything else to respect the dignity of the dead and the profundity of the mourning to which the dead called us. Indeed, I still try to heed that call for mourning and the future it promises because it recognizes the dignity of the dead, those who died on September 11, most certainly, but also those who have died as a result of the infinite war on terror. Like many who opposed the war, I expected the political scientist Richard Falk to support a solution to the threat posed by Al-Qaeda that did not include military action against Afghanistan. After all, Richard Falk has devoted his intellectual and political life to defending the ideal of humane global governance. He has been a life-long anti-militarist. Yet Falk supported the U.S. war against Afghanistan as a just war. Shortly after September 11, he wrote in *The Nation* magazine that "I have never since my childhood supported a shooting war in which the United States was involved."[1] But in the same article he goes on to claim that "[t]he war in Afghanistan against apocalyptic terrorism qualifies in my understanding as the first truly just war since World War II."[2]

Falk himself recognized that Al-Qaeda, because it was not a nation-state, challenged the very framework of just war and the process of legalizing war between states through international law that dates back several hundred years. Yet Falk sought to preserve the just war framework in order to temper the war on terror that has been pursued by the United States. As so many theorists and political commentators have noted, the war the United States declared completely rejected the conventional meaning of war. As famously defined by Clausewitz, war is politics by other means because war without a stated political goal would be senseless. An absolute war or, in Clausewitz's terms, an "ideal" war would be absolute only if it had no limitation, only a fight to the finish. But actual wars are always limited by the political interests that determine their possibility and desirability. For Clausewitz, the political goal of defeat emerges when the enemy asks for peace and is willing to submit to the victor.

Of course, much has changed since Clausewitz's time. But the idea that a war is declared by one nation-state against another or one group of nation-states against another has not been lost. Hence the problem of fighting a network in the traditional modern war system. To be sure, Falk understood that a war on terror could expand the meaning of war to such a degree that it is no longer limited by just war theory or other means of legalizing the limitations on war. To guard against this danger, he sought to redefine the meaning of winning and losing, making megaterrorism an exceptional form of terror and ultimately trying to maintain this war within the just war framework. The target for the war was twofold: Al-Qaeda's base in Afghanistan and the Taliban regime that supported those bases in Afghanistan. Making it clear that this would be a unique war, the Bush administration declared war on Afghanistan and at the same time declared that the United States was not at war with the Afghan people. That way, winning would not entail coercing the Afghan people to submit their will to the U.S. government. Rather, it would mean capturing the leaders of Al-Qaeda and completely destroying their base of operations in Afghanistan.

The Taliban was of course notorious for its crimes against humanity, particularly those committed against women. During the 25-year period prior to September 11, the Revolutionary Association of Women in Afghanistan (RAWA) had been pleading with the UN and the International Criminal Court and other international and transnational institutions, calling for intervention into the horrifying situation in Afghanistan first caused by the war the Soviet Union waged against the country. The pleas of RAWA were left unanswered except by small groups of feminists worldwide who tried to take up their cause. The Bush administration renamed its war effort a humanitarian invasion only after the ouster of the Taliban regime became its declared purpose of the war. Over the years, Falk has argued that we must be very careful about humanitarian invasions because these invasions often serve to further the economic interests of the most powerful countries. The Bush administration began to emphasize the humanitarian aspect of the war against the Taliban as Bin Laden and other key terrorist leaders increasingly eluded our forces. Falk never changed his position that a humanitarian invasion must proceed through the UN Security Council. Once the UN expanded the right to self-defense that the United States and other countries plagued by terrorism could claim, the question of the humanitarian invasion never arose for Falk. As a result, he did not try to defend the war on Afghanistan as a humanitarian invasion. Instead, he rather weakly referred to the "luck" that Bin Laden had been tracked in Afghanistan during the weeks immediately following September 11 to justify the invasion.

"[I]t was the apparent good fortune of the Bush administration," Falk claims, "that Osama Bin Laden had been operating from Afghanistan under Taliban rule in recent years, running a terrorist training program that apparently solicited tens of thousands of recruits from around the Muslim world in the aftermath of resistance to the Soviet presence throughout the 1980s. From the American perspective, Afghanistan was the ideal state to wage war against. It had practically no diplomatic friends in the world since the Taliban had come to power. On September 11, the Taliban government was recognized by only three countries in the world and has been refused the right to represent Afghanistan in the United Nations. Indeed, Afghanistan itself had been treated as an outlaw state for several years, a status confirmed by a special *rapporteur* appointed by the UN Human Rights Commission, who reported annually on the severe human rights abuses and crimes against humanity that were routinely taking place in the country, including massacres of ethnic minorities and horrifying impositions of an extreme version of the Sharia (Islamic Law) on Afghan women. As well, Afghanistan was the object of universal censure, including from Islamic governments, for its insistence on removing any taint of non-Islamic religious devotion by the deliberate destruction of the huge world-renowned statues of the Buddha at Budiman several months before September 11. If any state deserved the status of pariah or outlaw state, it was Afghanistan, even aside from the hospitality and free rein accorded to Al-Qaeda."[3]

But as Falk well knew, there is a big difference between declaring, as many feminists did around the world, that Afghanistan deserved to be an outlaw state and scrupulously enforcing such declarations through international law. Thus, even throughout his support of the war in Afghanistan, Falk remained committed to the humanitarian protections provided by international law and wary of military methods of achieving humanitarian goals. This is why he emphasized the *sui generis* nature of the Al-Qaeda threat. Indeed, Falk so narrowly defined megaterrorism as to ensure that almost no other organization would fit his definition: "Megaterrorism is violence against civilian targets that achieves significant levels of substantive as well as symbolic harm, causing damage on a scale once associated with large-scale military attacks under state auspices, and thus threatening the target society in a warlike manner that gives rise to a defensive urgency to strike back as effectively as possible."[4] Although we can certainly question whether Falk actually manages to limit his definition of megaterrorism, the limitation seems evident from his explicit concern that the UN legitimated U.S. claims of self-defense too haphazardly: "There was a rather casual and mechanical acceptance at the UN of the American claims, reflecting partly the sense that the Al-Qaeda attacks made all states vulnerable and sharing an interest in reducing the danger as quickly and effectively as possible. There was no reasoned discussion, much less debate, about why the charter should be interpreted as allowing reasonable measures of self-defense even in the absence of an armed attack as generally understood, or about the overall problem of dealing with threats posed by extremist political networks that operate transnationally. International law, which historically evolved over time to cope with relations among sovereign states, needs to be stretched to deal with megaterrorism, if it is to remain at all relevant. Nevertheless, I believe that the over-generalized U.S. approach to the megaterrorist challenge is dangerously serving to exempt state violence and policies from being regarded as terrorism—even when their violence is deliberately directed at civilian society. . . . This "anti-terrorist" bias weights the outcome of civic struggles in favor of the state and the status quo, depriving many peoples of the world of their fundamental right of self-determination."[5]

Despite his misgivings about the overly generalized U.S. response to the megaterrorist threat, Falk concluded that, "[u]nlike many anti-war activists who extended their condemnation of the Bush administration policies to include the Afghanistan military campaign, the limited war unleashed against the Taliban regime and the Al-Qaeda forces in Afghanistan seemed to me to be a reasonable extension of the right of self-defense in the context of a megaterrorist attack, and was so accepted by the Security Council, although less specifically and circumspectly than seems desirable, which would have included the identification of an applicable set of limits on these novel defensible claims."[6] But because Al-Qaeda was at once everywhere and nowhere, the irony was that the United States attacked a nation-state (although of course it insisted it was only attacking the Taliban regime) for its support of the Al-Qaeda terrorist network. Accordingly, the long-established relationship between the nation-state and war was both asserted and undermined. In Falk's mind, diplomatic efforts were impossible because of Al-Qaeda's authoritarian religious program, and the establishment of a transnational Islamic identity in which Islamic leaders become heads of existing nation-states in the Middle East. However, Falk admits that, despite Bin Laden's bombast and invective, the reputed leader of Al-Qaeda does have a political purpose, which at the very least is to overthrow the current regime in Saudi Arabia and to get the United States out of the Middle East altogether. But even in view of that purpose being political and not simply the result of Bin Laden's fundamentalist interpretation of *jihad*, Falk believed there was no room to negotiate over such sweeping demands. It was impossible and unrealistic, in other words, to demand that the United States simply end its military presence in the Middle East. "The visionary character of Bin Laden's worldview," Falk therefore argues, "suggests the primacy of non-specific goals such as the mobilization of the Islamic world in general. The terrorist pedagogy of Al-Qaeda and its practice up through September 11 add weight to an interpretation that stresses the goal of pushing the U.S. out of the region as a prelude to stepping up the pressures mounted on the established order in the Arab world, especially toppling the monarchy in Saudi Arabia."[7]

That Bin Laden never spoke of demands or of the possibility of negotiation only adds credence to Falk's position that negotiation was not a solution and that pacifists had to develop a solution. Falk also impugned the view that condemnations of U.S. imperialism and the violence it has unleashed on the world necessarily entails condemnations of any military action on the part of the United States. I wonder whether the view as Falk describes it is not something of a straw man attributable to a few sectarian groups in the peace movement that emerged in the wake of September 11. Still, to give Falk his due, he describes that position as follows: "Another form of anti-war advocacy rests on a critique of the United States as an imperialist super power or empire. This view also seems dangerously inappropriate in addressing the challenge posed by the massive crime against humanity committed on September 11. Whatever the global role of the United States—and it is certainly responsible for much global suffering and injustice, giving rise to widespread resentment that at its inner core fuels the terrorist impulse—it cannot be addressed so long as this movement of global terrorism is at large and prepared to carry out its demonic work. These long-term concerns—which include finding ways to promote Palestinian self-determination, the internationalization of Jerusalem, and more equitable distribution of the benefits of global economic growth and development to do so—must be addressed. Of course, much of the responsibility for the failure lies with the corruption and repressive policies of governments especially in the Middle East, outside the orbit of U.S. influence. A distinction needs to be drawn as persuasively as possible between inherently desirable lines of foreign policy reform and retreating in the face of terrorism."[8]

Falk is best understood to be making the case that foreign policy reform cannot be the sole solution to terrorism and, on that score, the vast majority of people in the worldwide peace movement would agree. I say this because Falk's own position regarding what constitutes the long-term "winning" of the war on terrorism presumes that we can actually make a clear-cut distinction between winning and losing. One alternative to foreign policy reform that Falk identified but rejected was the establishment of a special tribunal under UN authority. He argued that such an international tribunal would amplify the status of terrorists and thus be unable to deal with the very threat of terrorism it helped to perpetuate. He argued further that "[a] public prosecution would give Bin Laden and associates a platform to rally further support among a large constituency of sympathizers, and . . . it is doubtful that several of the permanent members of the Security Council could be persuaded to allow death sentences. Beyond this, the evidence linking Bin Laden to the September 11 attacks and other instances on global terrorism may well be insufficient to produce an assured conviction in an impartial legal tribunal, particularly if conspiracy was not among the criminal offenses that could be charged."[9]

When Falk began to voice public support for the war against Afghanistan, he arguably did not believe that the United States would support such a tribunal. Thus, because the United States would not accept an impartial legal tribunal, it was unrealistic to clamor for the establishment of one. Yet those who called for this sort of tribunal did not act with an eye toward what the United States would realistically do, but with an eye toward the ideals embodied in international law—the very ideals that Falk has spent his life working to articulate and defend. If we framed our ideals to be acceptable to the current administration in power, then they would be base indeed. No one, in the end, knows that better than Falk, which is why the most generous interpretation we can give to his recent work is that he wanted to keep the war against terror within the bounds of just war. After all, he emphasized that, whatever war is waged against the Taliban regime, it must be contained by the principles of just war, which for Falk are at least implicit in international law. These principles include:

> The principle of discrimination: force must be directed at a military target, with damage to civilians and civilian society being incidental; the principle of proportionality: force must not be greater than that needed to achieve an acceptable military result and must not be greater than the provoking cause; the principle of humanity: force must not be directed even against enemy personnel if they are subject to capture, wounded or under control (as with prisoners of war); the principle of necessity: force should be used only if nonviolent means to achieve military goals are unavailable.[10]

Although Falk's support for the war in Afghanistan seemed not to advance his earlier commitments to thinking about new forms of political community and affiliation at all levels, it did not completely undermine them either. In the main, his support was based on the following set of claims: "It is, above all, a war without military solutions. Indeed it is a war in which the pursuit of the traditional military goal of 'victory' is almost certain to intensify the challenge and the spread of violence. Such an assessment does not question the propriety of the effort to identify and punish the perpetrators and to cut their links to government power. . . . Acknowledging this legitimate right of response is by no means equivalent to an endorsement of unlimited force."[11] More recently, he has suggested that "whether U.S. behavior in the Afghanistan war should be regarded as satisfying the strictures of the just-war doctrine remains inconclusive, and it may remain so forever, certainly until more data and analysis is available."[12] If we take just war theory seriously, with its internal commitment to limiting non-combatant casualties, then one crucial way we judge that commitment is the extent of civilian casualties. Is the counting of civilian causalities, both in the numeric and moral sense, necessary to just war theory? One way we make a judgment about whether a war was fought justly is by evaluating the willingness of nation-states involved to accept greater risks for combat forces in order to save civilian lives.

Citing Donald Rumsfeld's notorious claim that there has never been a conflict with less collateral damage, less intended consequences than the war in Afghanistan, Falk accuses Rumsfeld of having an "impoverished imagination."[13] But the impoverishment of the moral imagination was part of how the war was fought. Indeed, the U.S. Government's refusal to record the number of causalities goes to the heart of whether the war was fought within the just war framework. Thus, I disagree with Falk when he claims that "allegations that civilian deaths in Afghanistan equaled or exceeded the number killed at the World Trade Center and Pentagon on September 11 seem unconvincing and are based on biased and unreliable evidence. . . . The issue is whether the violence used in self-defense was proportional to the harm inflicted and to a reasonable apprehension of future harm. It is hard to contend that the level of violence relied upon by the United States was disproportionately large in relation to the ends of restored security and punitive justice being reasonably sought."[14] On the one hand, just war theory assumes that because a nation-state can be legitimately attacked, the people of that state can be attacked with equal legitimacy. On the other hand, it assumes that just military operations will distinguish resolutely between military and civilian targets. So how do we assess the means used in retaliation when the terrible irony is that it was not the Afghan people we were retaliating against? The Bush administration was careful to claim that we were not at war with the people of Afghanistan. But if the United States really was not targeting Afghan civilians, there appears no justifiable way to legitimate as collateral damage the innumerable civilian casualties, especially when the U.S. military forces appeared to conflate military and civilian targets. How can we possibly evaluate the success of punitive justice when we still do not have at our disposal accurate figures that could confirm or deny that members of Al-Qaeda based in Afghanistan—and not Afghan civilians—were targeted?

Given Falk's criticism of Rumsfeld's impoverished imagination and the Bush administration's unwillingness to count civilian casualties and provide accurate information about them, it seems particularly paradoxical that he dismisses the information provided by sources outside the White House as biased and unreliable. After all, Falk has claimed that rather than forthrightly offering reliable statements about the means and ends of the war against terrorism, the Bush administration has instead generated propagandistic diversions that work to justify an untrammeled war against all networks, organizations, states, and peoples that challenge the economic and political interests of the United States. As he plainly asserts, "[T]he overall response to September 11 that has been enunciated and managed by the George W. Bush White House seems deeply flawed. The loss of focus has virtually precluded reasoned discourse on an effective, adaptive response to megaterrorism, and this loss has actually shifted the locus of discussion and action to other diversionary issues that pose high risks of their own (such as the propriety of recourse to war against Iraq)."[15]

Falk recognizes that the war in Afghanistan was itself a largely imprecise military campaign. The U.S. troops, he points out, relied on discredited weaponry—Vietnam B-52 bombing, cluster bombs, huge daisy cutter bombs containing 2000 tons of explosives—and made "mistakes on the ground" due to faulty intelligence information given by the Northern Alliance, hardly a stable alliance because the warlords that comprise it are always fighting for hegemony. Indeed, those mistakes, the result of internally divided groups of warlords trying to kill each other, actually led to civilian casualties. As everyone knows, many of the Al-Qaeda leaders, including Bin Laden, escaped and dodged the bombs. Perhaps fighter planes dropping bombs from 30,000 feet is not the most successful way to track criminals. But the question arises: does not carpet bombing flout the political and legal framework of just war by evidencing utter disregard for civilian causalities?

As we have seen, Falk disagreed with both anti-militarists and pacifists who argued that the United States cannot be granted an exceptional extension of the right to self-defense because it makes it too easy for the United States to extend such a right to all so-called forms of terrorism, not just the megaterrorism of Al-Qaeda. But at the same time, limiting military response to megaterrorism is part of how Falk thinks we can win the war. As he writes, "I take the position that war can be won only by a narrowing process that refocuses the defensive undertaking of the U.S. Government on Al-Qaeda. To the extent that global terrorism, as distinct from megaterrorism, is a legitimate concern on the part of target states, and it often is, then terrorism needs to be understood as political violence that is deliberately aimed at civilians and civilian society, whether perpetrated by political movements or by states. And even with such refocusing, a further process of clarification is necessary—namely, the limited role of military force in the war on global terror. Here again the Bush administration has been vague and indefinite, refusing to acknowledge any limitations on their recourse to force, unwilling to admit the relevance of international law or to allow a supervisory role for the United Nations. The U.S. Government has fashioned its policies on an ad hoc basis as it proceeds treating the goal and the scope of its military campaigns as matters purely to be determined by its own, non-accountable policy making. The impact of this approach is intensified by other related unilateralist moves: the rejection of widely endorsed international treaties on global problems, the refusal to transfer needed authority to international institutions, the insistence on its right to administer selectively the non-proliferation regime on the basis of its strategic interests, and the maintenance of cruel international sanctions on Iraq for years, despite the opposition of the great majority of members of the United Nations."[16] What rankles Falk to no end is that the Bush administration refuses to formulate policy, principles, or ideals as such; on the contrary, it constantly changes the goals, scope, and execution of its military and intelligence campaigns. On some level, Falk expects the Bush administration to endorse the ideals of just war, international law, and humane governance, even despite the fact that the Bush administration's entire public and foreign policy concerning terrorism (to say nothing of its views concerning the dissemination of accurate and reliable information) militates against those ideals.

Falk wrote *The Great Terror War* before the war against Iraq began, but at a time when Afghanistan had become a major battlefield in an endless war. Those of us who opposed the war in Afghanistan did so because we thought U.S. unilateral action was neither politically effective nor morally acceptable. Except for certain committed pacifists, most anti-war activists and intellectuals were searching for an effective and yet acceptable response to the terrorist attacks of September 11 and the global terror threat. Despite their many different principled liberal and left-wing positions, activists and intellectuals essentially agreed that the political effectiveness and moral acceptability of the response required that the Bush administration abide by the protocols of multilateralism. Jonathan Schell offers a compelling account of multilateralism:

> It is difficult to imagine the United States, acting alone or together with just a few nations, will be able to coerce or overthrow every regime that 'supports' terrorism or, for that matter, defeat or destroy every proliferator of weapons of mass destruction. The cooperation of governments, not their antagonism, is the indispensable precondition for a successful policy of opposing and reducing global terrorism of any kind. A cooperative policy

alone likewise avoids the danger, posed by the imperial approach, that hostile action, in the Middle East or elsewhere, will widen the pool of recruits for terrorist groups. At the same time, it is the likeliest basis for the political efforts that, over the long run, are the only lasting solution to terrorist threats.[17]

Activists and intellectuals who opposed the war in Afghanistan knew the political struggle against terrorism must endure for the long haul. Therefore, we thought it was important after September 11 to raise consciousness about the need for the United States to accept the political conditions of multilateralism that would have made possible a worldwide criminal investigation of Al-Qaeda and the establishment of an impartial criminal tribunal. But when Falk reduces the multilateralist position to nothing more than a narrowly political and legal commitment to an impartial criminal tribunal, he makes it seem that those who demanded police action as a proper response to the global terror threat were not serious about punitive justice. He gravitates dangerously close to dismissing idealists—whether activists, intellectuals, or political leaders—as necessarily and sufficiently unrealistic because they have no desire to be politically effective. But the call for multilateral action followed from a decidedly realistic commitment to political efficacy. Multilateralism simply means that, as a matter of principle, each nation-state should be accorded the dignity of its sovereignty by other nation-states, and treated with the same respect that the United States demands for itself and for its laws. Genuine multilateralism is inseparable from recognizing the political and legal centrality of the United Nations—an organization that continues to have as one of its long-term goals not only a full termination of inter-state wars and military conflicts, but also the end of war as a means of solving conflicts between sovereign nations. The political ideal behind the UN, if not its actual practice over the last few decades, is a form of federalism that secures the freedom of each state in accordance with international rights and affords each state an equal voice in the federation. Multilateralism requires that resolutions concerning nuclear disarmament must be followed, and that the ultimate decision as to what means of enforcement should be used against countries that breach such resolutions—Iraq, Syria, and North Korea are no exceptions here—must be reached by means of UN deliberation rather than by unilateral fiat. This means that the kind of arm-twisting, bullying, and leveraging that the United States practiced at the UN Security Council meetings in order to procure votes was wholly inappropriate in an international federation committed to maintaining an overlapping consensus of nations.

In view of multilateralism so understood, the United States is simply a state that should be accorded full respect like any other state—nothing less, but nothing more. Thus, on the level of international relations, it should seek to establish respect for the political integrity of all other states respect accorded to individuals by modern democratic constitutions (although admittedly, constitutions can take as many different forms as democratic regimes themselves). In the first instance, then, the United States should seek forms of conflict resolution consistent with international law through means other than war, rather than militarily defending its own naked economic and political interests. This means the United States should join an international criminal court—something it has consistently refused to do—and thereby show its commitment to the political ideals represented by international law. Moreover, the United States must involve itself in transnational agreements and accords that seek to solve problems unsolvable by any one nation-state. It is both politically unrealistic and morally repugnant for any state as powerful and wealthy as the United States to be isolationist. We should use the overwhelming crisis and historical trauma of September 11 to move the United States in the direction of multilateralism and away from the unilateralism and militarism that brought U.S. troops to Afghanistan and Iraq. What, after all, besides chaos and suffering, did the war bring to the people of Afghanistan and Iraq? As Iraqi people live under intolerable conditions, their resistance to U.S. occupation grows. And let us not forget the "state" of Afghanistan. Although billions of dollars in foreign aid have been allocated for the reconstruction of Afghanistan, organizations such as RAWA remain skeptical, arguing that this is not nearly enough to build an Afghan infrastructure and civil society capable of fostering and maintaining real democratic organizations and institutions. There is good reason for such skepticism because RAWA's dream of UN-supported governance and a true democratic rebuilding of Afghanistan has not been realized—not even close.

The war against Al-Qaeda has turned into an all-out war against every nation thought to harbor terrorists or weapons of mass destruction. Falk's distinction between terrorism and megaterrorism is collapsed nearly every day in major newspapers and during White House press conferences. Indeed, the distinction is now so elastic that it applies equally to megaterrorists and to Palestinians. Over the course of his career, Falk has argued that the Palestinians have the right to resistance and national self-determination due to the illegal occupation of the West Bank, which has been condemned endlessly by the UN. Yet to argue that the Palestinians have a right to resistance does not mean that one unflinchingly supports Hamas and its terrorist tactics. One can be morally against such tactics in general by simply appealing to the ideal of humanity and the dignity of each person. But Falk's point is that the inter-state political resistance bound up with the Palestinian struggle for self-determination should not be confused with the megaterrorism of Al-Qaeda. This conflation has allowed the United States to brand many Palestinian groups as terrorists because there is no Palestinian state supporting every violent action committed against Israel, whereas the state of Israel itself is fully behind every terrorist action against Palestinians. Falk seems right, then, to assert that the distinction between state terrorism and inter-state struggles that may involve actions against civilians should not be distinguished in such a way that disqualifies state action from being considered terrorism.

We know that the United States has included in the "axis of evil" not only inter-state groups who have their own political agendas against the states that harbor them, but also any state that might oppose the strategic interests of the United States. States might create a possible counter-deterrence to unconstrained U.S. aggression by developing effective weapons, regardless of whether they have engaged in aggressive action against the United States, or whether there is proof they harbor terrorist groups. Although Falk was vehemently opposed to the war in Iraq, he has failed to account for the vagary of self-defense, buttressed by just war theory rather than by international law, being used to justify the military invasion of Iraq. The U.S. hostility toward the UN Security Council was further evidence that, during the months in which the UN inspectors worked in Iraq, the United States had been preparing for war, making it very clear that it had no intention of following the UN if the UN did not support a U.S. preemptive strike against Iraq. The anti-militarists who were against the war in Afghanistan questioned the amorphous notion of self-defense, its possible misuse, and the ability of a state war to fight a transnational network. From the beginning, many of us involved in the anti-war movement have also mobilized against the USA PATRIOT Act, which curtails basic constitutional rights. This new legislation, which now includes homeland security and domestic security enhancement, is symptomatic of a new kind of war—a war with an endless horizon in which citizens must be policed by their own government in the name of security. At the same time, given the increased number of nations that can count as potential terrorist enemies, we have also seen the forced registration of legal residents who are from countries as diverse as Saudi Arabia and Pakistan. Such registrations are imposed on innocent people: the U.S. Government has no evidence of terrorist activity to marshal against them.

Returning to how U.S. political behavior actually enhances the plausibility of Bin Laden's accusations, the humiliation of legal residents only works to cast the United States as a sadistically strategic political actor on a rampage for control of the world's oil. Moreover, because the United States has considered departing from its position of using nuclear weapons only for deterrence, we have regrettably opened the door to a serious regression concerning the gradual movements toward non-proliferation that have occurred since the fall of the Soviet Union. In recent months, North Korea has proudly announced that it intends to proceed with its own nuclear program, and Iran has announced that it is considering pursuing its own attempts to develop nuclear weapons. Falk is very aware that the recent mobilization against the war in Iraq and the collapsing of all anti-state terrorism into megaterrorism has led the United States to return to the idea that, through its military power, it can control the rest of the world without having to consider any kind of deterrence. Will not the outcome be that, one by one, nation-states seek to protect themselves against an unrestrained superpower by developing themselves as counter nuclear powers? In Falk's view, we need to fight against the Bush administration's definitional confusions concerning inter-state terror and megaterrorism by showing how the war against terror might end. Ultimately, for Falk, the war can only come to an end if there is some kind of successful resolution of the conflict between Israel and Palestine in which actual negotiations with Palestinian leaders occur. We also need to come to grips with the number of Faustian bargains we have made in the Middle East (including with Saddam Hussein himself) and take responsibility for the legitimate grievances that countries and political groups within the Middle East have against the United States. Indeed, reconsideration of our policy in the Middle East, including our relationship to Israel, is an integral part of Falk's program for "winning the war." Falk also continues to think that the United States must relinquish its empire-building project and actually participate as one state among others in true multilateral political relations. He therefore identifies the ideal of multilateralism and respect for international law as crucial components of a successful strategy for "winning the war."

Although Falk supported the U.S. military campaign in Afghanistan, it is a mistake to think that he uncritically supports the infinite war on terror as pursued by the Bush administration. His sincerest hope was and remains the achievement of punitive justice against Bin Laden and Al-Qaeda. He tries to make it clear that this is his fundamental concern, by defining what he means by "losing the war": "My understanding of 'losing' is implicit in what I mean by 'winning.' Essentially, losing comes from treating the attacks in isolation from their social and political and cultural contexts, and reasserting as unambiguously as possible American hegemonic control over the Middle East, relying on direct and indirect means (that is, subordinated regimes, allies) and on military and non-military instruments of power, and pushing the world into a new phase of strategic rivalry by inducing reactions to an empire-building project undertaken behind the smokescreen of the war on global terror. Losing also means refusing to acknowledge the relevance of legitimate grievances, especially in the Arab world, but with respect to Islam generally, and even more broadly with respect to how the leadership role of the United States is exercised in world affairs. The targeting of the U.S. and Americans generally has not arisen in a political and moral vacuum, but against a background of perceived and actual abuse. . . . Losing is primarily understood in this analysis to mean a willful or negligent loss of focus on the September 11 threat, thereby embarking on a wider war than is legally or morally justifiable or necessary, with reliance on much more controversial benchmarks of effectiveness, and with the increased likeliness of a backlash effect arising from provoking both additional manifestations of extremism directed at the U.S. and its interests, and the stimulation of a drive by other countries to join together to contain what is regarded, with reason, as a U.S. bid for global dominance."[18]

Falk's rather singular redefinition of winning and losing takes us far beyond what we usually consider winning and losing; so much so that I would suggest that Falk does not ultimately agree with the designation of the fight against terror as a war, even despite his claim that the military strike against Afghanistan can be plausibly defended as a just war. Under Falk's terms, the United States is losing the war. Yet the United States seems to have no concept of losing other than ultimate defeat in global empire building. Quite rightly, Falk claims that "[e]fforts to re-empower the United States as the unchallenged hegemonic state actor seem to be accentuating the obsolete notions of statism rather than seizing the moment to move toward a truly empowering globalism that could protect all the peoples of the earth. In effect, contrary to first impressions, September 11 does not reaffirm the framework of a statist world order via the anti-terrorist undertaking led by the United States, but rather makes stark the choice for the peoples and elites of the world: global democracy or global empire."[19]

Along with multilateralism and international law, the ideal of humane governance is a central component for Falk's political strategy of dwarfing the giant terrorist networks and organizations that dot the globe. Let us examine Falk's own program for how that ideal might be realized. Throughout the 1980s and 1990s, Falk tried to tether his anti-militarism and anti-nuclearism to an avatar of post-modern ethics. There is much in this program that I accept, including the ideas that we must act as if the future were now and that we must be ready to journey to that future. "Within our zones of autonomous existence," he writes in *Explorations of at the Edge of Time*, "we can live as if our visionary hopes already exist and, by so doing, bring the desired transformation about. . . . Although we can model the future, we must not deceive ourselves that it is in place already. Such a pretension overlooks suffering and structures of domination and distortion; it facilitates escapist flights of fancy. The unifying struggle that informs reactions to various modernist failures is dedicated to the establishment of a non-violent, encompassing political community that allows distinct and diverse identities to flourish, overlapping and intersecting from individual to individual and group to group. It is not a specific project as such . . . but rather a perspective that animates action to the degree that over time a cumulative dynamic of transformation gathers force and eventually displaces the old superseded order . . ."[20]

But I cannot accept his extreme historical periodization of the modern, the pre-modern, and the post-modern. And neither should Falk. For he is trying to challenge the hierarchical models of history employed by the likes of Bernard Lewis, Frances Fukuyama, and Samuel Huntington—models that assert the superiority of Western civilization over and against the supposed darkness and evil of the Arab world. If we refuse to accept hierarchical conceptions of history and historical progress, then we need not sharply distinguish among the pre-modern, the modern, and the post-modern. On the contrary, we can recognize that the modern and modernity are fairly fluid historical forms. To his credit, Falk is willing to acknowledge such modern achievements as state-oriented democratization and the defeat of apartheid in South Africa. Furthermore, he accepts that new nation-states such as South Africa have played a crucial role in translating early human rights discourse, cynically deployed by the United States and the Soviet Union during the Cold War, into a normative political platform that can create new and viable challenges to U.S. political and economic domination throughout the world.

There is a sense in which Falk wants to claim that the post-modern world allows him to invert the civilization story as told by Fukuyama, Lewis, and Huntington (to say nothing of their epigones). Falk's thought is something like this: as the political and moral authority of nation-states decline, and as human beings seek transnational affiliations, some kind of normative replacement for what once could be found in the ideal of the modern nation-state must emerge. Falk believes there is something valuable about civilization thinking. It is evident to him that such thinking, when combined with religious traditions, may provide much richer grounds for the anti-military and anti-nuclear ideals he espouses. However, what Falk means by civilization is hopelessly vague. Sometimes, he seems to imply that civilization has a utopian aspect to it, meaning that we are striving to become more civilized in our behavior toward one another. At other times, he seems to indicate the transnational basis for civilizational identification, using

Islamic civilization as an example of the way in which culture, tradition, and history together form something with which people could identify across national boundaries. The danger here, however, is that Falk ends up reinforcing the fantasy that there are neatly circumscribed civilizations that must be separated if they are to provide the kind of regulative identification and normative guidance he seeks from them. Nevertheless, I share Falk's respect for the normative basis of human rights and anti-militarism that can be found in all the great religions. With him, I recognize the political and ethical dangers attendant upon an aggressive form of secularism that denies that very different comprehensive and general worldviews can agree upon programs of human rights, security, and transnational institutional structures. But unlike Falk, I think the best way to interrogate such secularism is by arguing against the linear learning process, often embraced by Hegelian historicists, that says Western modernity is the only model of modernity that can be followed or achieved.

Distinguishing the pre-modern, the modern, and the post-modern as he does, Falk may actually undermine his project of challenging the nation-state as the basis for politics. Rather than uplift his ideal of the citizen-pilgrim with its overzealous tones of a crusade and the danger of a politics of conversion, I would advocate embracing Étienne Balibar's ideal of civility as it relates to the symbolic universality of the ideal of humanity. Falk claims that the citizen-pilgrim "is on a journey in space and time, seeking a better country, a heavenly one. There are no illusions that the present is an embodiment of what is possible. The citizen-pilgrim is loyal to this quest and is not bound by any sense of duty to carry out the destructive missions of a given territorial state to which she or he owes temporary secular allegiance."[21] Unlike the pilgrimage of the citizen-pilgrim, civility helps us deal with the violence of our warring identities and affiliations; it demands as a political aspiration the space in which we can be other than how we currently identify and affiliate ourselves. "Civility," Balibar argues, ". . . is certainly not a politics that suppresses all violence; but it excludes extremes of violence, so as to *create* a (public, private) *space* for politics (emancipation, transformation), and enable violence itself to be historicized."[22] Both Falk's ideal of the citizen-pilgrim and Balibar's ideal of civility recognize the need to transcend narrow conceptions of national loyalty and exclusionary forms of ethnic racism imagined as the necessary basis for the constitution of a people. But Balibar does so without appealing to a kind of hyperbolic conversionist religious discourse that may be exclusionary in certain contexts. To be sure, Falk's pilgrim is not an easy figure to embrace, much less idealize, although admittedly he does want to extricate the pilgrim from its historical association with colonial America. While I am sympathetic to Falk's desire to connect the quest for anti-militarism to a more complex set of political identifications, I wonder about the extent to which Falk is willing to defend peace as a regulative ideal outside the framework of just war theory. Yet this is exactly what we need to advocate if we want the war on terror to reach its definitive end. For even as we recognize the need for preventive counter-violence in certain circumstances, we must always weigh the acceptance of such measures of preventive counter-violence against the ideal of peace itself.

Despite all of Falk's notable critiques of political realism and his insistence on anti-militarism as well as anti-nuclearism, he still refuses the ideal of peace as something that could provide us with a counter-framework to the legalization of war. This refusal is the result of his unwillingness to return to Immanuel Kant, who thought that we should dare to think peace as an ideal and that our natural history of unsocial sociability helps us approximate such an ideal. Just war theory has always operated as if it could keep war within certain limits and ensure that it proceed through certain principles, the most notable being non-combatant immunity defended by Michael Walzer.[23] But it is time to face the fact that there can be no such limitation unless nuclear weapons are outlawed altogether. Ironically, we need to accept that just war theory cannot survive the creation of nuclear weapons. Of course, some of its principles, such as noncombatant immunity, presume that nuclear weapons will not be used. Yet a weapon that exists always carries within itself the danger of being used. As Albert Einstein famously remarked, nuclear weapons have changed everything, except the way we think. Of course, they should change our thinking and make us commit ourselves to the ideal of perpetual peace. In light of multilateralism, after all, the disarmament of all states with nuclear power is a political necessity. As Jonathan Schell forcefully argues:

> An agreement to abolish nuclear arms and all other weapons of mass destruction is the *sine qua non* of any sane or workable international system in the twenty-first century. Any other attempted settlement of the issue of weapons of mass destruction will clash with efforts to bring peace, with common sense, and with elementary decency. No tolerable policy can be founded upon the permanent institutionalization of a capacity and an intention to kill millions of innocent people. No humane international order can depend upon a threat to extinguish humanity. Abolition alone provides a sound basis for the continued deepening and spread of liberal democracy, whose founding principles are violated and affronted by the

maintenance of nuclear terror: 'a democracy based on terror' is, in the long run, a contradiction in terms. And abolition alone can, by ending the nuclear double standard, stop proliferation and make effective the existing bans on other weapons of mass destruction. The logic of abolition is the real alternative to the logic of empire.[24]

No more than any other country does the United States need nuclear weapons—weapons of terror that cannot but perpetrate a horrifying death on a mass civilian population. The United States, then, does not need what is many times over the largest military force in the world—which is why we must oppose an ever-expanding debt economy capable of financing an infinite war. "[S]eeking help for the national economy from outside," Immanuel Kant wrote in his famous essay on perpetual peace, "or within a state . . . incurs no suspicion. But as machinery by which powers oppose one another, a credit system of debts growing out of sight and yet always secured against present demand . . . is a dangerous power of money, namely a treasury for carrying on war. . . . This facility in making war, combined with the inclination of those in power to do so . . . is therefore a great hindrance to perpetual peace. . . ."[25]

Given his spiritual bent, Falk often relies on the good intentions of people and on progressive national leaders to bring us closer to peace. I agree with him that human beings who invest in ideals are part of the process of changing the world. But Falk's own insistence that the reliance on war is always tragic goes beyond the claim of just war theory that the restraint of war is the beginning of peace. After all, the efforts at legalizing war may reinforce the very inevitability of war that prevents us from committing ourselves to the ideals of peace and humanity. Is commitment to the ideal of peace unrealistic and irrelevant? The brilliance of Kant was to see that just as a war between two nation-states can easily degenerate into a worldwide war, so the ideal of peace can bring together everyone in the world. For war, especially when conducted with weapons of mass destruction, is nothing but a destructive threat to the continuing survival of humanity. Thus, even a "race of devils" should be able to recognize the futility of war. Peace means "the end of all hostilities," Kant argued, "and to which it is already a suspicious pleonasm to attach the adjective *perpetual*. . . . A condition of peace among men living near one another is not a state of nature (*status naturalis*), which is much rather a condition of war, that is, it involves the constant threat of an outbreak of hostilities even if this does not always occur. A condition of peace must therefore be *established*. . . . Nations, as states, can be appraised as individuals, who in their natural condition (that is, in their independence from external laws) already wrong one another by being near one another; and each of them, for the sake of its security, can and ought to require the others to enter with it into a constitution similar to a civil constitution, in which each can be assured of its right. This would be a *league of nations* . . ."[26]

In his extraordinary essay entitled "The Idea of Humanity and the Project of Universal Peace," Claude Lefort explicitly endorses the thinking of peace rather than the endless legalization of war that currently holds so much intellectual sway. "[P]eace," he writes, "can be based only on the idea that the relationships among men are relationships among fellow men. It follows, then, that this idea is not unconnected with that of freedom. It also follows that it would be hypocritical to countenance, in the name of peace, every form of exploitation of peoples who see themselves, under cover of the laws of the market, deprived of the resources of their territory and subjected to an overt or disguised form of dictatorship: it would be hypocritical, too, to countenance every form of totalitarianism that denies elementary rights to individuals and to minorities."[27] The kind of peace that Lefort envisions could easily include forms of preventive counter-violence. But peace, like all regulative ideals in Kant, is irreducible to a goal. So arguments that we have never achieved peace cannot be used to distort the dream of perpetual peace. The ideal of peace must guide our actions no less than our thinking. It must inform how we think and act beyond the frameworks of just war theory and political realism even as just war theorists continue to uplift legal restraints on the conduct of war as the best we can do. So let us all listen carefully to Lefort's stirring admonition concerning peace:

> Mindful not to succumb to utopian thinking and careful to take into account the exigencies of the contemporary world, let us not confuse the cause of peace with an unprincipled pacifism. But, mindful of reality, let us not succumb, either, to the dizzying spectacle of current conflicts. Let us recognize, rather, that the sovereigns do not decide alone the fate of humanity . . . and that, far from being futile, the silent work of rapprochement among men, which takes place with the aid of increased mutual mores and mentalities, progress of education, the spread of information, and the rise of the idea of human rights, can engender decisive effects of a political order heading in the direction of peace.[28]

Returning to Falk for the last time, it is important to remember that, throughout his work in political science and international relations, Falk has called upon us to perform work of rapprochement. He has insisted that such work cannot proceed unless we can project a horizon of hope into the future. After the historical trauma of September 11, many Americans in the United States wanted to give up on that hope. Alarmist news reports about increasing terror levels, coupled with sensationalist and extremist political invective emerging daily from the White House, made it seem that the worst was yet to come. Everyday people and citizens were not given the chance to mourn and pay heed to the dignity of the dead. So let us now give each other that chance to mourn and take back the future from trauma no less than from terrorism. Through our weeping and our tears, we must let the ideal of perpetual peace lead us to a better world.

Variegated Visions of Humanity: John Rawls' "The Law of Peoples"   3

When John Rawls first published his essay entitled "The Law of Peoples," many of his liberal admirers were confused by his argument that liberalism, no matter how broadly defined, cannot be the general and comprehensive worldview for the law of peoples and more sweeping proposals for global justice. His commitment to the history of political philosophy always led him to insist that there were many liberalisms, not just one that was the true way of liberalism. But both in the essay and the revised monograph, *The Law of Peoples*, that followed, he goes beyond the claim that there is a plurality of liberalisms to insist that a law of peoples must not be based in liberal principles; otherwise, it would be much too narrow and deny equal standing before such a law to many of the world's peoples who do not live in liberal societies.[1]

The law of peoples for Rawls is a political conception of justice and right that would apply to the principles and norms of international law and international institutions. Today, Rawls' insistence on the need for a law of peoples seems prescient in its concern about the hegemonic aspirations of the United States in the world and what they might mean for democracy in the United States. The events of 9/11 may make some consider Rawls' "realistic utopia"[2] in the form of a law of peoples seem outdated. Rawls himself did not explicitly write about the events of 9/11, since his monograph was published in 1999, but he addresses the need to stay true to a course that allows for hope in the face of what he calls "demonic possibility."[3] As Rawls reminds us in the face of horrific world events, devastating wars, and outright genocide: "we must not allow these great evils of the past and present to undermine our hope for the future of our society as belonging to a Society of liberal and decent Peoples around the world. Otherwise, the wrongful, evil, and demonic conduct of others destroys us too and seals their victory. Rather, we must support and strengthen our hope by developing a reasonable and workable conception of political right and justice applying to the relations between peoples."[4] His creation of an idealized Islamic people in his attempt to outline the contours of a "decent hierarchical people," which he called "Kazanistan,"[5] shows Rawls' determination to counter the pervasiveness of negative stereotypes about the Muslim religion.

Of course, Rawls' worry about the hegemonic aspirations of the United States and his concern to promote a fair view of the Muslim peoples were not the only things that motivated him in developing a law of peoples. From the beginning of his philosophical journey, Rawls argued that justness as fairness, once it had secured the principles of justice within a just and democratic nation-state, should extend such principles to international law and institutions. The elaboration of the law of peoples was always central to Rawls' conceptualization of how societies must have some understanding of themselves in relation to each other. What is crucial for Rawls is that a constructivist doctrine proceeds first by generating principles of justice for a self-contained democratic society. In his famous account, this is done by placing free and equal citizens in an original position behind a veil of ignorance where these idealized representatives— idealized because they are presumed to be both free and equal—deliberate about what principles and institutional structures they would adopt if they had general relevant information but did not know their own specific interests or their place in the hierarchies of class, race, and gender in any given society. Because the process is represented as fair, in that the idealized representatives are not guided in their deliberations by their vested interests, the outcome of their deliberations is considered to be just. Rawls offers five features of the original position in his formulation of it in *The Law of Peoples*. "Here, five features are essential: (1) the original position models the parties as representing citizens fairly; (2) it models them as rational; and (3) it models them as selecting from among available principles of justice those to apply to the appropriate subject, in this case the basic structure. In addition, (4) the parties are modeled as making these selections for appropriate reasons, and (5) as selecting for reasons related to the fundamental interests of citizens as reasonable and rational."[6] Rawls argues in his early work, *A Theory of Justice*, that such representatives would adopt two principles. The first principle is the priority of the right over the good, which would allow citizens to pursue their own ideas as to what the good life is. A second principle, Rawls' famous difference principle, limits the first principle. It is a principle of equity that argues that all citizens' behavior would have to operate under a presumption of equality in which the only inequalities allowed would be those that benefited the worst off in society. Rather than address whether these two principles of justice can actually be derived from the original position—a question that has fueled much debate among political philosophers—I want to emphasize the constructivist experiment in the imagination that Rawls envisions as fair. For it is the representational device of the veil of ignorance within the original position that Rawls uses to develop a law of peoples.

The limit on constructivism inheres in the way in which it proceeds subject by subject rather than by seeking a comprehensive principle. More precisely, the sequence of the subjects addressed places a limit on the questions that can be asked. The first use of the original position, for example, in domestic society actually abstracts from relations with other societies. Thus, at the level of domestic society, questions crucial to the law of peoples are not even asked and would be denied if the subject addressed were domestic society.

At the heart of Rawls' conception of the political is the idea that a law of peoples should not rest on any general and comprehensive worldview and therefore must be free-standing in relationship to any such worldview that encompasses all the subjects that are most pressing to human beings, including life, death, and love. On the contrary, a law of peoples should refer to the basic institutions and norms of international law. In the original essay version of "The Law of Peoples," Rawls, from the outset, offers reasons concerning why he begins with a law of peoples rather than with a global original position: "Wouldn't it be better to start with the world as a whole, with a global original position, so to speak, and discuss the question whether and in what form, there should be states, or peoples, at all? . . . I think there is no clear initial answer to this question. We should try various alternatives and weigh their pluses and minuses. Since in working out justice as fairness I begin with domestic society, I shall continue from there as if what has been done so far is more or less sound. Thus I build on the steps taken until now, as this seems to provide a suitable starting point for the extension to the law of peoples. A further reason for proceeding thus is that peoples as corporate bodies organized by their governments now exist in some form all over the world. Historically speaking, all principles and standards proposed for the law of peoples must, to be feasible, prove acceptable to the considered and reflective public opinion of peoples and their governments."[7]

All of Rawls' claims concerning universality proceed by extending the representational device of the veil of ignorance within the original position and what it should mean for the questions at hand. His fundamental concern is that his law of peoples not be historicist, but in a specific sense; that is, he wants it to be applicable to liberal societies but not just to them alone. He wants to take into account historical formations of peoples that may not even assume the historically recognizable form of the liberal nation-state and yet could still be counted as a people. If the law of peoples were only acceptable to liberal peoples, it would not be universal. By universal, Rawls means inclusive of all peoples of the world who could feasibly accept such a law without having to fit the dominant mold of certain Western liberal societies. Universal thus means scope—all the peoples of the world—and conditions of acceptability, which leads Rawls to argue that at least certain kinds of what he calls "decent hierarchical societies" would agree to extend the veil of ignorance and the original position to themselves in their relations to other societies. Rawls' essay has troubled some of his most liberal readers because he tries to show that an overly confident and complacent liberalism, in the context of international law, ironically courts a lack of tolerance or respect for other societies that do not have liberal institutions or a liberal self-understanding.

Rawls seeks a parallel of reasonable pluralism within a politically liberal society to a law of peoples: "In the Society of Peoples, the parallel to reasonable pluralism is the diversity among reasonable peoples with their different cultures and traditions of thought, both religious and nonreligious. Even when two or more peoples have liberal constitutional regimes, their conceptions of constitutionalism may diverge and express different variations of liberalism. A (reasonable) Law of Peoples must be acceptable to reasonable peoples who are thus diverse; and it must be fair between them and effective in shaping the larger schemes of their cooperation."[8] Although Rawls usually speaks of tolerance, the spirit of both his essay and his monograph is more consistent with a stronger notion of respect because any supervisory role of liberal societies over those deemed non-liberal is discounted at the level of the ideal. Yet those who deeply believe in the superiority of both the liberal way of life and liberal theories of justice are not discounted in turn. For that would belie Rawls' own commitment to respecting the general and comprehensive worldviews of others and their alternative conceptions of justice. This means that, from the perspective of the Law of Peoples, acknowledging the legitimacy of different worldviews requires the concomitant acknowledgment of different theories and practices of justice—even certain hierarchical ones that are non-liberal: "A main task in extending the Law of Peoples to nonliberal peoples is to specify how far liberal peoples are to tolerate nonliberal peoples. Here, to tolerate means not only to refrain from exercising political sanctions—military, economic, or diplomatic— to make a people change its ways. To tolerate also means to recognize these nonliberal societies as equal participating members in good standing of the Society of Peoples, with certain rights and obligations, including the duty of civility requiring that they offer other peoples public reasons appropriate to the Society of Peoples for their actions."[9]

More specifically, Rawls thinks that respect should be directed toward religious peoples who do not accept the separation of church and state— a separation that, for some political philosophers, is part of the very foundation of liberalism. Perhaps more than ever before, today we are confronted with the question of respecting religious peoples who do not assume the traditional liberal form. "There is a question about religious toleration," Rawls claims, "that calls for explicit mention. Whereas in hierarchical societies a state religion may be on some questions the ultimate authority within society and control government policy on certain important matters, that authority is not . . . extended politically to other societies. Further, their (comprehensive) religious or philosophical doctrines are not unreasonable: they admit a measure of liberty of conscience and freedom of thought, even if these freedoms are not in general equal for all members of society as they are in liberal regimes. A hierarchical society may have an established religion with certain privileges. Still, it is essential to its being well-ordered that no religions are persecuted, or denied civic and social conditions that permit their practice in peace and without fear."[3]

Rawls' defense of a principled entry of "decent hierarchical societies" into a law of peoples stems from his recognition that although the very notion of sovereignty has changed, how and when we can override sovereignty is exactly what makes the law of peoples so pressing. Rawls explicitly states that the role and reach of international law is greater now than ever since World War II. At the heart of the change is the acceptance that limits must be imposed by international law, limits on state sovereignty itself, including the right to use military force. Further, the role of human rights today is much more significant in actual international covenants, treaties, and institutions. These are two very basic historical changes for Rawls, and a law of peoples must recognize their significance.

Let us return now to the original position as Rawls uses it to imagine the moment of judgment in which liberal societies (and then decent consultation hierarchical societies) place themselves behind the veil of ignorance with the law of peoples as the subject before them. Liberal peoples follow many different blueprints of liberalism. There are, however, three features they must maintain: (1) a basic list of rights and opportunities, (2) a high priority of these fundamental freedoms, and (3) legal and economic measures that enable people to make use of their freedom. Following the procedure for domestic societies, but now with international relations before him, Rawls argues for several crucial limits on information behind the veil of ignorance that would be imposed upon these societies. The five features of the first original position are now remodeled for the second. "Thus, people's representatives are (1) reasonably situated as

free and equal, and peoples are (2) modeled as rational. Also their representatives are (3) deliberating about the correct subject, in this case the
content of the Law of Peoples. (Here we may view that law as governing
the basic structure of the relations between peoples.) Moreover, (4) their
deliberations proceed in terms of the right reasons (as restricted by a veil
of ignorance). Finally, the selection of principles for the Law of Peoples is
based (5) on a people's fundamental interests, given in this case by a liberal conception of justice (already selected in the first original position).
Thus the conjecture would appear to be sound in this case as in the first.
But again there can be no guarantee."[10] Some of the right reasons Rawls
refers to in (4) are the following: they know the general and favorable conditions that make democracy possible, but they do not know the extent
of their natural resources, the level of their economic development or their
actual military power. They also do not know the size of their territory
or their population. To try to answer the criticism that the representatives
are situated as free and equal and thus are being postulated as members
of a liberal society, Rawls argues that the representatives in this original
position are not taken as free and equal individuals, but as free and equal
peoples in a society of peoples. Thus, his second original position could
be acceptable to decent hierarchical societies because it does not presume
any philosophical view of the person. Further, because liberal societies,
under Rawls' understanding of liberal, do not have a general and comprehensive worldview that is imposed upon the government and basic
institutions, liberal societies too could endorse the second original position although it does not endorse a specifically liberal view of the person.
Rawls' reasonable hope is that with these restrictions on information,
liberal peoples would endorse the following eight principles:

> 1. Peoples are free and independent, and their freedom and independ-
> ence are to be respected by other peoples. 2. Peoples are to observe
> treaties and undertakings. 3. Peoples are equal and are parties to the
> agreements that bind them. 4. Peoples are to observe a duty of non-
> intervention. 5. Peoples have the right of self-defense but no right to
> instigate war for reasons other than self-defense. 6. Peoples are to honor
> human rights. 7. Peoples are to observe certain specified restrictions in
> the conduct of war. 8. Peoples have a duty to assist other peoples living
> under unfavorable conditions that prevent their having a just or decent
> political and social regime.[11]

It is the principle of non-intervention that is particularly crucial for
understanding why Rawls does not simply start from the nation-state and
then gravitate toward some kind of multilateral system of cooperation
based on prudential interest.

Rawls held the optimistic belief that actual democratic societies are unlikely to wage war with each other because, in a democracy, the people themselves know they have the power to make decisions and that they will bear the burden. Here he is surprisingly radical: he argues that some wars by so-called democratic states are neither democratically nor legitimately decided due to the oligarchic tendencies that frequently lead governments to pursue the interests of a few capitalists. Therefore those wars do not count against his basic presupposition that a democratic society would have integral constraints on the pursuit of war. Rawls argues that certain military actions of the United States do not disprove his presuppositions about war and democracy, because they were wars in defense of oligarchic interests. "Witness the United States' overturning the democracies of Allende in Chile, Arbenz in Guatemala, Mossadegh in Iran, and some would add, the Sandinistas in Nicaragua. Whatever the merits of these regimes, covert operations against them can be carried out by a government bureaucracy at the urging of oligarchic interests without the knowledge or criticism of the public, and presenting it with a *fait accompli*. All this is made easier by the handy appeal to national security given the situation of superpower rivalry in the Cold War, which allowed these democracies, however implausibly, to be cast as a danger. While democratic peoples are not expansionist, they do defend their security interest, and this an oligarchic government can easily manipulate in a time of superpower rivalry to support covert interventions once they are found out."[12] Had Rawls lived, I think he would have added to his list of wars waged for oligarchic interests the recent war against Iraq. In any case, we can see more fully why Rawls believes that his law of peoples functions in accordance with actual changes in sovereignty and why Rawls is so concerned with having a law of peoples in the first place.

Rawls believes that through the veil of ignorance and the original position we are generating, at least on the level of the hypothetical imagination, a socially adjusted world envisioned as a law of nature that necessarily guides our transformative action within the extant world. For Rawls, this imaginative experiment helps us represent principled limits on what had been taken to be the laws of nature, including our nature, prior to their idealization and universalization in the original position itself. This, precisely, is why it is a mistake to think of the veil of ignorance within the original positions, either the first or second, as defined in *The Law of Peoples*, and the constraints on information they demand, as reducible to our ignorance of what place we are to assume in already existing hierarchies within societies or between peoples of the world. Often, Rawls is thought to forbid us knowledge of our places in the great lotteries of life as these allocate such identities and positions as class, race, and gender. But the lottery metaphor fails to grasp the central significance for Rawls of the move from an adjusted social reality that acts upon our nature to a world we are morally demanded to re-imagine and transform such that grossly unequal societies and relationships between peoples would no longer exist.

From within the adjusted social reality imposed by the law of peoples, state sovereignty is always already imagined as limited by such reality. This is indeed why Rawls himself uses the word "peoples" rather than "nation-states". As Rawls explains, "[t]hus, in working out the Law of Peoples, a government as the political organization of its people is not, as it were, the author of all of its own powers. The war powers of governments, whatever they might be, are only those acceptable within a reasonable Law of Peoples. Presuming the existence of a government whereby a people is domestically organized with institutions of background justice does not prejudge these questions. We must reformulate the powers of sovereignty in light of a reasonable Law of Peoples and deny to states the traditional rights to war and to unrestricted internal autonomy."[13] Therefore, on the level of the ideal, there would not be any superpowers as we now know them, because the very notion of a superpower flagrantly rejects the law of peoples.

Without understanding the ideality of the adjusted social reality, it is difficult to understand the two conditions under which the veil of ignorance can properly function as a representational device—the publicity and perpetuity condition. By the publicity condition, Rawls means that there must be public recognition of the laws of peoples as they are developed in the procedure. The perpetuity condition allows Rawls to defend an equilibrium state that could ultimately be reached as the result of an adjusted social reality that achieves what he describes as rightful stability over time, including stable and peaceful relationships between nation-states. Some of Rawls' critics and interlocutors, including Amartya Sen, point out that an equilibrium state may actually undermine Rawls' more radical insistence that we are always defending a reasonable faith in the power of ideals to regulate and direct the way in which we struggle to change our world.

Here I do not so much want to answer this criticism as emphasize why, on Rawls' account, we seek something like the projection of the ideal over time. For Rawls, in the conduct of war in a non-ideal world, we still seek to achieve an effective and lasting equilibrium that certain means of war are simply unjustifiable any time, any place. Rawls was one of the few Anglo-American philosophers of his time who passionately condemned the use of nuclear weapons in Hiroshima and Nagasaki. It was not right, under any version of just war theory or for any reason, to use nuclear weapons in this situation. If we judge an action by a nation-state to be unjust in the means chosen for war, we should be able to sustain the projection of that judgment back in time as regulative of our behavior in the future, unless of course conditions change enough that they demand the reformulation of the ideal itself. Thus, perpetuity is the eternity that Rawls associates with the ideal of universality, which demands that the process of judging ideals is simultaneously the projection of those ideals back and forth through time and history. His earliest formulation of this point can be found in *A Theory of Justice*: "The perspective of eternity is not a perspective from a certain place beyond the world, nor the point of view of a transcendent being; rather it is a certain form of thought and feeling that rational persons can accept within the world. And having done so, they can, whatever their generation, bring together into one scheme all individual perspectives and arrive together at regulative principles that can be affirmed by everyone as he lives by them, each from his own standpoint."[14]

Only this projection of ideals back in time as part of the process of arriving at regulative principles can lead to the reformulation of ideals. But Rawls' point is that we must also have an ability to judge our history in accordance with ideals that we may only formulate after the fact. Rawls, then, is concerned with what might be called moral memory: remembering our own histories differently once we have performed the labor of self-reflection that the commitment to idealism demands. As Rawls claims in his essay entitled "Fifty Years after Hiroshima," "We should be able to look back and consider our faults after fifty years. . . . It can't be that we think we waged the war without moral error."[15] If a previous war was unjust, if a means deployed in a war was unjust, then from the viewpoint of the ideal and the limit it imposes on us, we must take responsibility for that injustice as citizens of the United States, even those currently living who may not have been born during the time of Hiroshima and Nagasaki. The viability of ideals turns on our responsibility for defending them. For history in Rawls always means as much of a moral engagement with what we project into the future as into the past.

Although Rawls himself is not a pacifist—and indeed defends some retention of nuclear weapons as long as there are outlaw states—he offers an important consideration of the role of pacifism in both a just society and in the law of peoples. Like Immanuel Kant, Rawls is very much guided by the ideal of perpetual peace. But if peace is indeed an ideal, then it means not only that certain limits will be placed on war, but that its very ideality will shape the way we imagine those limits in accordance with the bounds of national sovereignty. There are no empires under the law of peoples that can pursue their "oligarchic" interests without full democratic participation in war (assuming war is necessary for reasons of self-defense). Pacifists are closely allied with just societies because they work to promote justice as fairness even if they do not describe their commitment as necessarily political. Rawls defends the right of pacificists to express their position against all war and to believe that it is part of their general and comprehensive worldview to do so. Of course, it could be argued that at some point the pacifist must concede to the public principles of an imagined just society because those principles are themselves inclusive of those that guide just war theory. But Rawls' point is that pacifists can actually play a role in bringing the people of any given nation-state closer to the ideal of peace. Rawls is only too well aware—as Kant was—of the "realist" pressure and aspirations that can lead nation-states awry politically when they enter the fray of history as superpowers with unimaginable military power.

As he claims, "If pacifism is to be treated with respect and not merely tolerated, the explanation must be that it accords reasonably well with the principles of justice, the main exception arising from its attitude toward engaging in a just war (assuming here that some wars of self-defense are justified) the political principles recognized by the community have a certain affinity with the doctrine the pacifist professes. There is a common abhorrence of war and the use of force, and a belief in the equal status of moral persons. And given the tendency, particularly of great powers, to engage in war unjustifiably and to set in motion the apparatus of the state to suppress dissent, the respect accorded to pacifism serves the purpose of alerting citizens to the wrong that governments are prone to commit in their name. Even though his views are not altogether sound, the warnings and protests that a pacifist is disposed to express may have the result that on balance the principles of justice are more rather than less secure. Pacifism as a natural departure from the correct doctrine conceivably compensates for the weakness of men in living up to their professions."[16]

Rawls clearly believes that members of a just society would abhor war. As a soldier in World War II, Rawls experienced the horrors of war first-hand and was deeply moved by them. It is precisely this aversion to war in a just and democratic society that can be easily eclipsed in a nation-state that does not fit the constraints of Rawls' theory of justice and his law of peoples. But Rawls goes further than just defending pacifism. He vehemently defends the politics of conscientious refusal within any given nation-state or people as necessary, irrespective of whether the society in question is just according to his principles of justice. No matter how close we might come to the ideal of justice, we would still need such a politics. Pacifism must be defended as a crucial ally in the struggle for justice not only because we do not yet live in a just world, but also because we live in a world in which the global peace movement is mocked and condemned by the current administration of the United States.

Rawls resolutely connects the politics of conscientious refusal and civil disobedience: civil disobedience is always directed to political change, while conscientious refusal may only be an appeal to moral exemption. However, as a litmus test for liberalism, the distinction is not important; and given the recent attacks on the peace movement, we clearly must insist on the political significance of both. Arundhati Roy reminds us why: "Any government's condemnation of terrorism is only credible if it shows itself to be responsive to persistent, reasonable, closely argued, nonviolent dissent. And yet what is happening is just the opposite. The world over, nonviolent resistance movements are being crushed and broken. If we do not respect and honor them, by default we privilege those who turn to violent means. Across the world, when governments and the media lavish all their time, attention, funds, research, space, sophistication, and seriousness on war talk and terrorism, then the message that goes out is disturbing and dangerous: If you seek to air and redress a public grievance, violence is more effective than non-violence. Unfortunately if peaceful change is not given a chance, then violent change becomes inevitable."[17] Roy eloquently testifies in much of her writing to the role that religious hatred and persecution have played in India. Rawls' persistent call for religious tolerance was inspired by the recognition that religion, as Roy reminds us, is so often the source of violence.

Rawls thinks that any decent peoples, including liberal peoples, must find principles to confront the reality that there are many different religions in the world, some of which come to assume leadership positions in nation-states. His is a lone voice, within certain liberal circles, in seeking to defend as a matter of principle those societies that are not recognizably liberal because they do not institutionally and legally incorporate the separation of church and state. Rawls defines decent hierarchical societies as having three necessary features. The first is that they do not seek to expand their own religious conception of life to other societies. If a certain religious creed does seek wider influence, it can only do so in ways that do not interfere with other peoples' civic orders and conceptions of liberties and rights. A creed, on Kant's account (and Rawls is following Kant here), is a religious point of view that, broadly defined, worships the order of things by having faith that our place in the universe is part of God's work and thus worthy of reverence and devotion. Of course, not all creeds deeply believe that they are the only true way to God. For Rawls, a creed that has such a belief institutionalizes itself hierarchically by conferring its members with privileges that followers of other creeds do not receive.

But this assertion of the supremacy of a religious creed is only permissible if it does not involve the persecution of other religions. This means that worshippers of other faiths cannot be denied citizenship and must be granted the space for their respective religious practices. Rawls recognized that even in 1999, there was a deep suspicion of the Muslim religion as being unable to provide the conditions for what he calls a "decent, hierarchical society." He tried to counter that image of the Muslim religion by imagining an idealized Islamic people—Kazanistan. To quote Rawls, "Kazanistan's system of law does not institute the separation of church and state. Islam is the favored religion, and only Muslims can hold the upper positions of political authority and influence the government's main decisions and policies, including foreign affairs. Yet other religions are tolerated and may be practiced without fear or loss of most civic rights, except the right to hold the higher political or judicial offices. (This exclusion marks a fundamental difference between Kazanistan and a liberal democratic regime, where all offices and positions are, in principle, open to each citizen.) Other religions and associations are encouraged to have a flourishing cultural life of their own and to take part in the civic culture of the wider society."[18] Rawls daringly describes this idealized people as interpreting *jihad* as a spiritually inspired ethical ideal rather than in military terms, making an important intervention into the reigning prejudice that *jihad* is necessarily a declaration of war. *Jihad*, interpreted as a spiritual ideal, is something akin to the kingdom of God that could actually promote inclusion of diverse religions in the Muslim state. As Rawls states, "[t]o try to strengthen their loyalty, the government allows that non-Muslims may belong to the armed forces and serve in the higher ranks of command. Unlike most Muslim rulers, the rulers of Kazanistan have not sought empire and territory. This is in part a result of its theologians' interpreting *jihad* in a spiritual and moral sense, and not in military terms. The Muslim rulers have long held the view that all members of society naturally want to be loyal members of the country into which they are born; and that, unless they are unfairly treated and discriminated against, they will remain so. Following this idea has proved highly successful. Kazanistan's non-Muslim members and its minorities have remained loyal and supported the government in times of danger."[19] The idea that a particular creed can believe itself to be the only way to God and yet accept these limitations is not such a difficult notion to accept on Rawls' account. He thinks that one can believe wholeheartedly in one's own general and comprehensive worldview but nonetheless recognize that there are other people who believe deeply in their own. This goes even for certain academic liberals who believe that their general and comprehensive worldview is the one true way, if not to god, then to the best possible secular order. But just as political liberalism must temper itself by appealing to its own internal convictions and set of ideals, so must the great religions, including those obviously different from the Christianity espoused by a good many liberals.

The second feature of decent hierarchical societies is that they recognize certain basic human rights. The third feature of such societies is that they adopt what Rawls calls a common good conception of law. Rawls rejects the argument that a legal system *qua* legal system must be founded upon principles of public and private rights including individual autonomy—principles purportedly integral to its claim to validity. Nonetheless, he does believe that, if law is to be accepted as such, it must publicly embody some degree of impartiality: that is, judges must take into account the interests of all members of society, and their moral duties and obligations must be defined by some set of acknowledged standards that seem reasonable to the parties involved in conflict, religious or otherwise. Just as this kind of impartiality can only be hoped for if the hierarchical society possesses mechanisms for consulting with the different groups that comprise it, so there must be institutions such as corporate bodies and assemblies that can effectively represent divergent interests. Here, Rawls follows Hegel: "A first observation concerns why there are groups represented by bodies in the consultation hierarchy. (In the liberal scheme, separate citizens are so represented.) One answer is that a decent hierarchical society might hold a view similar to Hegel's, which goes as follows: in the well-ordered decent society, persons belong first to estates, corporations, and associations—that is, groups. Since these groups represent the rational interests of their members, some persons will take part in publicly representing these interests in the consultation process, but they do so as members of associations, corporations, and estates, and not as individuals. The justification for this arrangement is as follows: whereas, so the view goes, in a liberal society, where each citizen has one vote, citizens' interests tend to shrink and center on their private economic concerns to the detriment of the bonds of community, in a consultation hierarchy, when their group is so represented, the voting members of the various groups take into account the broader interests of political life. Of course, a decent hierarchical society has never had the concept of one person, one vote, which is associated with a liberal democratic tradition of thought that is foreign to it, and perhaps would think (as Hegel did) that such an idea mistakenly expresses an individualistic idea that each person, as an atomistic unit, has the basic right to participate equally in political deliberation."[20]

For Rawls, it is plausible to presume that these minimum conditions can be met without imposing grandiose liberalism as the only basis for the law of peoples and that this plausibility is enough to allow for the extension of the veil of ignorance within the original position to hierarchical societies. If hierarchical societies endorsed the law of peoples, the endorsement would include human rights, given their commitment to consultation and to impartiality defined by a common good theory of law. Indeed, Rawls thinks a common good theory of law that recognizes its members as cooperative social participants acting in accordance with moral duties and obligations is all that is necessary for a society to endorse human rights broadly conceived. On Rawls' view, human rights thus do not turn on any strong conception of human nature. Instead, they are one of two universalizable lessons learned from the historical experience of World War II. The second lesson, as we have already seen, is the limit of the external exercise of coercive authority through war, even when deployed as a means of self-defense.

Still, we are left with these questions: how can we engage with other non-liberal people? How can we do so in the Rawlsian spirit of toleration and respect? Rawls invites us to answer these questions by undertaking what, in his very late writing, he calls conjectural reasoning. He associates reasoning by conjecture with the duty of civility in a politically liberal society. This duty starts with our respect for others as reasonable, rational, and equal in their ability to listen and reflect. Rawls suggests in his essay entitled "The Idea of Public Reason Revisited" that "we argue from what we believe, or conjecture, are other people's basic doctrines, religious or secular, and try to show them that, despite what they might think, they can still endorse a reasonable political conception that can provide a basis for public reasons. The ideal of public reason is thereby strengthened. However, it is important that conjecture be sincere and not manipulative. We must openly explain our intentions and state that we do not assert the premises from which we argue, but that we proceed as we do to clear up what we take to be a misunderstanding on others' part, and perhaps equally on ours."[21]

Some have argued that the veil of ignorance demands that we imagine ourselves in as many different positions as possible—positions such as race and gender that are social realities. But what Rawls actually demands is that we imagine an adjusted social world as if it were currently a law of nature and could direct us in how we envision the ideals and principles that would be central to that world. He therefore does not call us to imagine what it is actually like to be in someone else's shoes. The self-reflective nature of conjectural reasoning inveighs against the presumption that we can ever use our moral or political imagination in that way. What we can do, however, is imagine that someone who may seem very strange to us is reasonable and rational and that the experience of strangeness must not be translated into a judgment of inferiority. Western societies are thus asked to at least presume the responsibility for and accountability to the people of consultation hierarchical societies and to educate themselves enough about different religions and cultures so that those who live in liberal societies can eventually hazard imaginative conjectures about others that are also reasonable and rational. We must expand the notion of reasonableness if we are to engage respectfully with hierarchical societies. We can do this by recognizing others as responsible members of their societies who are able to articulate their moral commitment to certain social values. But without the presumption imposed by the duty of civility, we are unlikely to undertake this moral and political education because we imagine that we already know. At the heart of the burden of judgment for Rawls is that we all confront the consequences of our prejudiced attitudes toward other general and comprehensive worldviews. Because Rawls himself wants to undertake this kind of critical confrontation, he hesitates to adopt an expansive concept of cosmopolitan right, one that might be envisioned through a global original position.

As a result, Rawls is careful not to define human rights from within a general and comprehensive liberal worldview. For Rawls, human rights are limit principles imposed by the law of peoples. Their status as limit principles defines their role in the law of peoples and their role defines their content. For Rawls, human rights have three roles:

"1. Their fulfillment is a necessary condition of the decency of a society's political institutions and of its legal order. 2. Their fulfillment is sufficient to exclude justified and forceful intervention by other peoples, for example, by diplomatic and economic sanctions, or in grave cases, by military force. 3. They set a limit on pluralism among peoples."[22]

The procedure by which particular rights are adopted by peoples would have to be taken into account in any established federation of peoples. And the process of universalizability would involve imagining how other peoples would agree to limit their sovereignty by the extension of human rights behind the veil of ignorance. Because it presumes an already existing law of peoples, this process transcends the kind of multilateralism that takes given nations-states as its point of departure. Such multilateralism lacks the ideality of a law of peoples. Thus, a nation-state that tried to define its sovereignty outside these limits would be an outlaw regime. A law of peoples thus promotes international federations such as the UN because states both limited and defined by that law would seek to honor it and promote respect for it. It gives us an ideal basis for multilateralism and offers us an explanation of why unilateral humanitarian intervention defies this law by definition.

But we are clearly not living in a world that is guided by the ideal of the law of peoples. Rawls considers two problems in our non-ideal world: (1) non-compliance with international law and (2) unfavorable conditions, of what he calls "burdened societies." Writing in the 1990s, Rawls was acutely aware of the fact that we are far from having a law of peoples by which all of the world's people actually abide. In its preemptive strike against Iraq and non-compliance with the UN Security Council, the United States made such a law seem even more distant and unattainable. But this makes it all the more important to define the conditions in which just war against an outlaw regime—such as Saddam Hussein's—is legitimate and justified. Rawls is succinct and profound on this point: "The law-abiding societies—both liberal and hierarchical—can at best establish a *modus vivendi* with the outlaw expansionist regimes and defend the integrity of their societies as the law of peoples allows. In this situation the law-abiding societies exist in a state of nature with the outlaw regimes, and they have a duty to their own and to one another's societies and well-being, as well as a duty to the well-being of peoples subjected to outlaw regimes, though not to their rulers and elites. These several duties are not all equally strong, but there is always a duty to consider the more extensive long-run aims and to affirm them as overall guides of foreign policy. Thus, the only legitimate grounds of the right to war against outlaw regimes is a defense of the society of well-ordered peoples and, in grave cases, of innocent persons subject to outlaw regimes and the protection of their human rights. This accords with Kant's idea that our first political duty is to leave the state of nature and submit ourselves along with others to the rule of a reasonable and just law."[23]

Unfavorable conditions in "burdened societies" are the product of the overwhelming poverty in which so many of the world's people live. Rawls does not defend as part of his law of peoples a global difference principle or any other liberal principle of distributive justice. Indeed, some of Rawls' most thoughtful egalitarian commentators have accused him of insensitivity and even moral indifference to the horrible suffering of people in the global south. Their accusation is a response to the following notorious passage in Rawls: "I would further conjecture that there is no society anywhere in the world—except for marginal cases—with resources so scarce that it could not, were it reasonably and rationally organized and governed, become well-ordered."[24]

But Rawls here is not indifferent or insensitive to suffering at all. Instead, he proffers guidelines to help us in providing assistance so that all societies would be able to meet the basic needs of their peoples and secure their human rights. The first guideline is based on an interpretation of a just savings principle. The savings principle within *A Theory of Justice* was to impose limits on consumption, and the use of capital and natural resources, such that any current generation could not leave the generations to follow completely bereft of their conditions for flourishing. But in the course of applying this principle to the law of peoples, Rawls is implicitly challenging the idea that efficiency in the form of achievement of the greatest possible development of the gross national product can or should be imposed on societies by the United States which largely controls such powerful international organizations such as the International Monetary Fund and the World Bank. These institutions often impose what gets called structural adjustment against immediate spending on social services in the name that such spending does not save enough capital for direct investment in development defined as the speediest possible increase in the gross national product. In other words, Rawls is refusing the idea that wealth in and of itself is the goal of assistance. Rawls' position challenges that of mainstream development economics, which argues that all societies must adopt the Western capitalist model of economic growth if they are to flourish. He understands that an unflagging commitment to a mode of economic development based on the capitalist market system can be coercive both economically and culturally in its delivery of certain "assistance packages" and certain dominant Western liberal values. The second guideline demands that we look carefully at how we might assist "burdened societies" so as to change their political and cultural conditions in order to prevent terrible disasters such as famines, and ultimately to ensure that the neediest people actually receive the packages of assistance that are meant for them.

Rawls is concerned that "each people be treated as a full and self-standing member of the society of peoples, capable of taking charge of their political life and social institutions."[25] The third guideline is actually a reinforcement of the first. To quote Rawls; "The third guideline for carrying out the duty of assistance is that its aim is to help burdened societies to be able to manage their own affairs reasonably and rationally and eventually to become members of the Society of well-ordered Peoples. This defines the "target" of assistance. After it is achieved, further assistance is not required, even though the now well-ordered society may still be relatively poor. Thus the well-ordered societies giving assistance must not act paternalistically, but in measured ways that do not conflict with the final aim of assistance: freedom and equality for the formerly burdened societies."[26]

Given the nature of these two guidelines, Rawls would not be able to accept the corporatist original position advocated by Leif Wenar, although Wenar is deeply sympathetic to the law of peoples and its attempt to limit the coercive and military power of the nation-state.[27] Indeed, Wenar agrees with Rawls that we cannot simply step beyond the law of peoples and move toward a global egalitarian order based on a global original position. But he thinks that the law of peoples must be supplemented by a corporatist original position that would generate ideals capable of regulating international economic institutions. Wenar's thought is that representatives in the form of producers, owners, and consumers should be placed behind the veil of ignorance and attempt to regulate economic institutions that the law of peoples does not directly address. Although consumers, producers, and owners are positioned to recognize their particular interests as divergent from those of the other groups, each group is to be regarded fairly, with all their interests being of equal worth. Wenar recognizes that his veil of ignorance is "thinly stitched" and may seem to introduce too much reality (and hence not enough ideality) in the way the interested groups are named. Although Rawls himself does not explicitly address the corporatist addition to the law of peoples, he does seem to grant implicitly that naming the representatives in this way concedes too much to the reality of market-driven capitalism on the level of the ideal. The first and third guidelines are meant to provide limits on market-driven capitalism as it is taken to be a model or and ideal for development.

Rawls grapples with poverty and suffering by trying to understand it as a political problem that requires a political solution. He reminds us that many of the world's poorest peoples are actually quite rich when it comes to natural resources. In his second guideline, Rawls worries, however, about the effect of political corruption of elites within those societies—corruption that often prevents people from being able to claim their own "riches," whether natural or cultural. As Rawls insists, "[W]hat is so often the source of the problem [is] the public political culture and its roots in the background social structure. The obligation of wealthier societies to assist in trying to rectify matters is in no way diminished, only made more difficult. Here, too, in ways I need not describe, an emphasis on human rights may work, when backed by other kinds of assistance, to moderate, albeit slowly, oppressive government, the corruption of elites, and the subjection of women."[28] The point of the three guidelines is to set a target, to bring "burdened societies" to the point where they could determine their own fate. This emphasis on self-determination serves as a limit to what kind of aid can be provided and how it can be delivered. "I also suggest that it is not reasonable for a liberal people to adopt as part of its own foreign policy the granting of subsidies to other peoples as incentives to become more liberal, although persons in civil society may raise private funds for that purpose. It is more important that a liberal democratic government consider what its duty of assistance is to peoples burdened by unfavorable conditions. I shall also argue later that self-determination, duly constrained by appropriate conditions, is an important good for a people, and that the foreign policy of liberal peoples should recognize that good and not take on the appearance of being coercive. Decent societies should have the opportunity to decide their future for themselves."[29]

Human rights could play an important role in a political solution, but only if they are not implicated in a general and comprehensive liberal worldview. How, then, can human rights be expanded in a direction acceptable to Rawls and still have some actual political force in international law and in transnational institutions? We can address this question by considering Thomas Pogge's argument that "a human right is fulfilled for some person if and only if this person enjoys *secure access to the object of this human right*. Here the *object* is whatever this human right is a right to—adequate nutrition, for example, or physical integrity. And what matters is *secure access* to such objects rather than these objects themselves, because an institutional order is not morally problematic merely because some of its participants are choosing to fast or to compete in boxing matches."[30] Pogge's argument is that how we judge a society or people is ultimately dependent on whether objects of human rights are actually secured for them. It is the security of these rights and not an actual list upon which Pogge focuses. This leads Pogge to emphasize certain kinds of responsibilities and duties imposed on the wealthier countries which prevent them from blocking the creation of a global political order to secure human rights. This understanding of human rights, which still primarily makes them rights against existing governments, also carries within it the demand for new international and transnational institutions that would make this security possible for all peoples. Indeed, the demand for such a global order is how Pogge interprets The Universal Declaration of Human Rights, which reads "Everyone is entitled to a social and international order in which the rights and freedoms set forth in this Declaration can be fully realized."[31]

Pogge's defense of responsibility for political and economic elites in the wealthier countries is consistent with Rawls' own emphasis on corruption as central to the problem of poverty. Pogge emphasizes that the international borrowing privilege can feed corruption because it allows certain elites to borrow money and use money in ways that do not benefit the people at large and then pass on their debts to the next elected government. Examples of problems with the borrowing privilege are legion in South America and Africa. This privilege, of course, is unthinkable without the major economic institutions of the World Bank and the International Monetary Fund. For Pogge, the wealthiest nations control these institutions and therefore control the terms of the borrowing privilege. On his account, these nations also control the international resource privilege. As Pogge describes this privilege, "[It] includes the power to effect legally valid transfers of ownership rights in such resources. Thus a corporation that has purchased resources from the Saudi or Suharto families, or from Mobuto or Sani Abacha, has thereby become entitled to be—and *is*—recognized anywhere in the world as the legitimate owner of these resources. This is a remarkable feature of our global order. A group that overpowers the guards and takes control of a warehouse may be able to give some of the merchandise to others, accepting money in exchange. . . . Contrast this with a group that overpowers an elected government and takes control of a country. Such a group, too, can give away some of the country's natural resources, accepting money in exchange. In this case, however, the purchaser acquires not merely possession but all the rights and liberties of ownership, which are supposed to be—and *are*—protected and enforced by all other states' courts and police forces. The international resource privilege, then, is the power to confer globally valid legal ownership rights in the country's resources."[32] Pogge thinks that our current global economic order would be unthinkable without wealthier regimes constantly supporting corrupt regimes. This leads him to conclude that citizens in the wealthier countries are responsible for the promotion of an international order that furthers corruption.

Here we can bring Pogge's account of human rights to bear on Rawls' insistence that aid must always be given in such a way that tolerates and accepts the diverse ways of life embodied in the law of peoples. Pogge's concern that wealthier societies have promoted corruption through direct or indirect coercion is perfectly consistent with Rawls' concern that non-ideal circumstances often times are cited as justification for delivering "aid" in such a way that undermines the law of peoples. Recognizing that the international economic order is pervaded by the brutal reality of economic inequalities encouraged by the promotion of corrupt regimes and that the wealthier nations play a role in such promotion, we may actually be able to envision new means of economic rectification that promote Rawls' interest in fostering tolerance and respect. This would further help us recognize "aid" as part of the process of a people achieving full standing as free and equal.

Still, the question remains: does the law of peoples need to be supplemented by a broader understanding of transnational justice—including an expanded conception of human rights—and the ideal of humanity? Rawls' formulation of human rights has the advantage of relying upon nation-states for the ultimate support and enforcement of such rights. Thus, there is no problem of coherence: where there is a right, there is a duty to enforce that right. In other words, for a right to exist, there must be an exact correlation between right and obligation. Two consequences follow from this: (1) human rights establish a demand for effective mechanisms of enforcement, and (2) we must re-think the human as it is figured in any conception of human rights so understood. Given both their history and their moral potential, can human rights also plausibly be interpreted as making a demand for realization irreducible to perfect obligation? Amartya Sen has recently answered in the affirmative: "It is . . . possible to resist the claim that any use of rights except with co-linked perfect obligations must lack cogency. In many legal contexts that claim may indeed have some merit, but in normative discussions rights are often championed as entitlements or powers or immunities that it would be good for people to have. Human rights are seen as rights shared by all—irrespective of citizenship—the benefits of which everyone *should* have. While it is not the specific duty of any individual to make sure that the person has her rights fulfilled, the claims can be generally addressed to all those who are in a position to help. Indeed, Immanuel Kant has characterized such general demands as 'imperfect obligations' and had gone on to discuss their relevance for social living. The claims are addressed generally to anyone who can help, even though no particular person or agency may be charged to bring about the fulfillment of the rights involved."[33]

Imperfect duties can be interpreted as a call to form complex transnational organizations that not only promote a political and legal culture in which human rights can actually be secured, but also open up space for cultural and political contestation of the very status of humanity as that which can be conferred in the form of a legal right. Typically there are two ways of thinking about human rights: (1) one tethers such rights to a supposedly given or readily accessible human nature; (2) the other defends them as conferring a status of humanness that can be negotiated and contested. The latter is more consistent with Sen's emphasis on our freedom to challenge, as a matter of political struggle, conceptions of humanity that have served as the very basis for certain legal entitlements to human rights. Indeed, freedom as contestation over the ideal of humanity is what Sen ultimately seeks to defend as an ethical and political extension of the law of peoples. As he claims, "Even the identity of being a human being—perhaps our most basic identity—may have the effect, when fully seized, of broadening our viewpoint, and the imperatives that we may associate with our shared humanity may not be mediated by our membership of collectivities such as 'nations' or 'peoples'."[34] Yet how are we to seize this identity—humanity—precisely by contesting it? Part of the answer is that by working in transnational organizations, we must necessarily (although not always sufficiently) confront the divergence between identifying simply as a human being (identification that thereby attempts to transcend the mediation of nationality, race, or ethnicity) and being positioned as a superior or inferior human being given one's nationality, race, or ethnicity.

Sen seems to recognize that we all have identifications and positions. He understands the importance of grappling with identities and positions that are frequently contradictory and even at variance with each other. As he explains, "For example, a doctor could well ask what kind of commitments she may have in a community of doctors and patients, where the parties involved do not necessarily belong to the same nation. It is well to remember that the Hippocratic oath was not mediated—explicitly or by implication—by any national or international contract.

Similarly, a feminist activist could well consider what her commitments should be to address the special deprivation of women in general—not necessarily only in her own country. There may well be conflicting demands arising from different identities and affiliations, and these respective demands cannot all be victorious. The exercise of assessing the relative strength of divergent demands arising from competing affiliations is not trivial, but it would beg a very large question if we were to deny our multiple identities and affiliations just to avoid having to face this problem. The alternative of subjugating all affiliations to one over-arching identity—that of membership of a national polity—misses the force and far-reaching relevance of the diverse relations that operate between persons. The political conception of a person as a citizen of a nation—important as it is—cannot override all other conceptions and the behavioral consequences of other forms of group association."[35]

Sen thinks we can undertake this difficult task of recognizing the diverse relations between people (relations informed by a multiplicity of identities and positions) by enlisting the help of Adam Smith's impartial spectator who can arbitrate between two parties. Although the spectator could be imagined as impartial through a Rawlsian constructivist experiment in the imagination, I do not think such a spectator really captures Sen's nuanced understanding of identity and position. Finding a reasonable and rational means of impartially arbitrating the conflict between two warring identities is not the issue. After all, many of us regularly undertake such arbitration as participants in actual political organizations and struggles. Thus, it is best to imagine that we are conjectural participants in such arbitration processes. We conjecture about the meaning of our participation not only as a matter of how we identify ourselves within a given organization or struggle, but also as a matter of how we are identified by others within an organization or struggle, given our actual positions in the world of social, political, and economic hierarchies. Only by working to accept our diverse identities and positions—political and ethical labor that must be performed through our commitment to the law of peoples—can we begin to struggle through what it means to be a conjectural participant in our variegated visions of humanity.

Developing Human Capabilities: Freedom, Universality, and Civility 4

Economic development as an ideal is inextricably linked to the ideal of progress. But can it be unmoored from the developmental narrative of nation-building and the civilizing mission of triumphant market-driven liberalism? I want to answer by suggesting that we have no choice but to expand the meaning of development as freedom. In this regard, Amartya Sen's work in political liberalism and development economics is indispensable. Sen's thought retains a spirit of both Kantian and Marxian radicalism by privileging freedom as both the means and end of development. Sen departs from triumphant market-driven liberalism in the name of the very value of freedom that it ostensibly promotes. His departure is consistent with a Rawlsian defense of the law of peoples and the advancement of human rights. But to enlist Sen—as Martha Nussbaum does—in the promotion of a list of specific human capabilities as the basis of human rights is to undermine Sen's insistence on the centrality of freedom.

On May 22, 1979, Sen delivered a Tanner Lecture at Stanford University entitled "Equality of What." The lecture was primarily a critique of the Rawlsian conception of justice as the equal distribution of primary social goods—goods such as rights, liberties, opportunities, income, and wealth. "The primary goods approach," argued Sen, "seems to take little note of the diversity of human beings. . . . Rawls takes primary goods as the embodiment of advantage, rather than taking advantage to be a relationship between goods and persons."[1] He argued further that, within the Rawlsian framework, "what is missing . . . is some notion of 'basic capabilities': a person being able to do certain basic things . . . the ability to meet one's nutritional requirements, the wherewithal to be clothed and sheltered, the power to participate in the social life of the community. . . . [E]ven though the list of [primary] goods is specified in a broad and inclusive way . . . it still is concerned with good things rather than with what these goods do to human beings."[2] Interpreting needs in the form of basic capabilities led Sen to endorse basic capability equality. But it does not follow, as some would have it, that Sen's initial formulation of the capabilities approach was a purely negative response or corrective to Rawls' theory. On the contrary, as Sen himself admitted in 1979, "[t]he focus on basic capabilities can be seen as a natural extension of Rawls' concern with primary goods, shifting attention from goods to what goods do to human beings."[3]

Throughout the 1980s and 1990s, in a series of important articles and books that bridged the gap between development economics and liberal political philosophy, Sen defended equality of well-being as the answer to the question concerning "equality of what?". His core idea was that this form of equality could be measured by the actual level of well-being achieved by human beings living in different societies under different conditions. His critique of competing liberal theories of equality, many of which relied on thin distributive theories of justice, was that they could not account for the real diversity among human beings. One such theory is Ronald Dworkin's, which argues (at least in one formulation) that "any conception of equality that respects ethical individualism must aim to make people equal, not in well-being judged from some collective point of view, but in the resources each controls. In a society that is egalitarian in that sense, people are free to decide how to use their equal share of resources to achieve higher well-being or a better life as they judge that, each for himself or herself. Equality of resources, in other words, is a liberal conception of equality."[4] On Sen's account, the thinness of this sort of conception of equality is that it does not consider how the equal sharing and redistribution of resources affect a person's ability to make judgments and decisions about his or her freedom in relation to a particular level of well-being. Contra Dworkin and others, Sen began to define well-being in terms of a person's capability to function and achieve a certain quality of life. Through a theory of human functioning, he deepened his early account of basic capability equality. He develops this theory of functioning in *Inequality Reexamined*, where he argues that "[l]iving may be seen as consisting of a set of interrelated 'functionings,' consisting of beings and doings. A person's achievement in this respect can be seen as the vector of his or her functionings . . . [which are] constitutive of a person's being, and an evaluation of well-being has to take the form of an assessment of these constituent elements. . . . The relevance of a person's capability to his or her well-being arises from two distinct but interrelated considerations. First, if the achieved functionings constitute a person's well-being, then the capability to achieve functionings . . . will constitute the person's freedom—the real opportunities—to have well-being. . . . The second connection between well-being and capability takes the direct form of making achieved well-being itself depend on the capability to function."[5]

Whereas functioning sets compare and contrast the well-being of different human beings, capability sets focus explicitly on the freedom to achieve valuable functionings. "Capability," Sen therefore claims, "is primarily a reflection of the freedom to achieve valuable functionings. It concentrates directly on freedom as such rather than on the means to achieve freedom, and it identifies the real alternatives we have. In this sense it can be read as a reflection of substantive freedom. Insofar as functionings are constitutive of well-being, capability represents a person's freedom to achieve well-being."[6] Over the years, Sen has retained the name "capabilities approach" for his conception of development precisely because it prioritizes capabilities over functionings. For, in his view, people across the world should have the greatest possible freedom and capability to achieve functioning sets—bundles of beings and doings—that give value and meaning to their lives. More recently, however, Sen's focus has been less on capability and functioning sets than on substantive freedom itself. Indeed, by the time he was a Fellow at the World Bank in the late 1990s, Sen had simply defined freedom as the means and end of development. Hence his claim in *Development as Freedom* that "[t]he analysis of development presented in this book treats the freedom of individuals as the basic building blocks. Attention is thus paid particularly to the expansion of the "capabilities" of persons to lead the kind of lives they value—and have reason to value."[7] What might have previously been called deprivation of functioning sets thus gets rephrased as peoples' desperate need to be freed from the worst forms of unfreedom. "Very many people across the world," Sen declares, "suffer from varieties of unfreedom. Famines continue to occur in particular regions, denying to millions the basic freedom to survive. Even in those countries which are no longer sporadically devastated by famines, undernutrition may affect very large numbers of vulnerable human beings. Also, a great many people have little access to health care, to sanitary arrangements or to clean water, and spend their lives fighting unnecessary morbidity, often succumbing to premature mortality."[8]

In Sen's view, human beings can extricate themselves from the worst forms of unfreedom by having untrammeled access to five instrumental freedoms: political freedom, economic facilities, social opportunity, transparency guarantees, and protective security. Sen justifies the instrumentalism of these freedoms by showing the integral link between each freedom in particular and the enhancement of human freedom in general. In this way, the five freedoms function as individual means toward the end of substantive freedom. This justification of the instrumental freedoms is inseparable from Sen's insistence that our basic perspective must be that of the actual agents of development. But as Sen reminds us, "[t]he use of the term 'agency' calls for a little clarification. The expression 'agent' is sometimes employed in the literature of economics and game theory to denote a person who is acting on someone else's behalf (perhaps being led on by a 'principal'), and whose achievements are to be assessed in the light of someone else's (the principal's) goals."[9] Against the grain of contemporary economics, Sen's conception of agency is such that the agent "is someone who acts and brings about change, and whose achievements can be judged in terms of her own values and objectives, whether or not we assess them in terms of some external criteria as well."[10] He concerns himself, then, with "the agency role of the individual as a member of the public and as a participant in economic, social, and political actions, varying from taking part in the market to being involved, directly or indirectly, in individual or joint activities in political and other spheres."[11] Regarding the five instrumental freedoms, Sen asserts that they all work in tandem to maintain and strengthen each other. Political freedoms include free speech, religious tolerance, and, more especially, the ability to participate in all areas of political and civil society, including the governmental bodies and NGOs that purport to serve peoples' best interests. Social opportunities—*inter alia*, the ability to achieve literacy and a certain minimum level of bodily health—allow people to work and become productive members of society. Economic facilities not only help individuals generate personal wealth, but also help to develop the necessary public resources for facilities like schools and hospitals because they are meant to provide gainful employment to the largest possible number of people in any given situation.

Economic facilities are Sen's most potentially radical freedoms, although to date he has kept their definition close to more traditional economic ideas such as access to markets, credit, and other means of forming businesses and even cooperatives. How far Sen might be willing to push his conception of economic facilities toward a conception of workplace democracy and even political contest over the meaning and nature of work itself remains an open question. Arguably, however, his conception of economic facilities is in keeping with the need to rethink the role of markets and Marx's fundamental argument that redistribution of goods would never work under a capitalist market system as long as the processes of production and the circulation of value did not radically change. Of course, unlike Marxists, Sen thinks that markets can play a role not only in the economics of development, but also in the politics of emancipation and transformation. Yet it is important to note that Sen views markets as one institution among many within a diverse array of institutions. He claims, after all, that individuals "live and operate in a world of institutions. Our opportunities and prospects depend crucially on what institutions exist and how they function. Not only do institutions contribute to our freedoms, their roles can be sensibly evaluated in the light of their contributions to our freedom. To see development as freedom provides a perspective in which institutional assessment can systematically occur. Even though different commentators have chosen to focus on particular institutions such as the market or the democratic system or the media, or the public distribution system, we have to view them together, to be able to see what they can or cannot do in combination with other institutions. It is this integrated perspective that the different institutions can be reasonably assessed and evaluated."[12] To be sure, Sen is neither a Marxist nor a socialist. But the capabilities approach can be open to the critical examination of the production of goods—the role of workers' cooperatives, for example—and the enhancement of economic opportunities that corrects for a one-sided attention to the distribution of goods. This allows Sen to depart from distributive theories of justice à la Rawls in which mere access to primary goods becomes at once necessary and sufficient for the end of substantive freedom.

Transparency guarantees are indispensable for political freedom and economic facilities because without them human beings are not able to make sound judgments: opaqueness blocks the flow of information that allows for meaningful ethical and political debate about the best possible society that can be developed and how such development can be achieved. Sen envisions transparency guarantees as giving people "the freedom to deal with one another under guarantees of disclosure and lucidity. When that trust is seriously violated, the lives of many people . . . may be adversely affected by the lack of openness."[13] Protective security is needed, Sen suggests, "to provide a social safety net for preventing the affected population from being reduced to abject misery, and in some cases even starvation and death. The domain of protective security includes fixed institutional arrangements such as unemployment benefits and statutory income supplements to the indigent as well as ad hoc arrangements such as famine relief or emergency public employment to generate income for destitutes."[14]

This agency-centered conception of freedom allows Sen to depart from dominant paradigms of development (many of which are still prevalent in the recent economic and political discourse of the World Bank). These paradigms use abstract normative criteria to judge the stages of development and modernity. Their judgment and evaluation of development conform to what Sen calls "some unique and precise 'criterion' of development in

terms of which the different development experiences can always be compared and ranked."[15] Against this criterion-driven model of development
analysis, Sen rightly points out that "[g]iven the heterogeneity of distinct
components of freedom as well as the need to take note of different persons' diverse freedoms, there will often be arguments that go in contrary
directions. The motivation underlying the approach of 'development as
freedom' is not so much to order all states—or all alternative scenarios—
into one 'complete ordering,' but to draw attention to important aspects
of the process of development, each of which deserves attention. Even after
such attention is paid, there will no doubt remain differences in possible
overall rankings, but their presence is not embarrassing to the purpose
at hand."[16] Unlike the dominant economic focus on delivery packages
of goods, services, and strategies for lesser-developed countries to enter
the competitive fray of global markets, Sen's progressive paradigm of
development considers the developmental stages in which the multitudi-
nous unfreedoms currently plaguing large cross-sections of the world's
population can be overcome. In a passage that echoes the historical mate-
rialist philosophy of Karl Marx, Sen argues that "[t]he process of development . . . is not essentially different from the history of overcoming
these unfreedoms. While this history is not by any means unrelated to
the process of economic growth and accumulation of physical and human
capital, its reach and coverage go much beyond these variables."[17]

Perhaps more clearly than any other moment in Sen's work, these
words betray Sen's commitment to development as something like the
ideal historical project in which human beings realize and give meaning
to their freedom as such. That this project possesses a certain ideality means
that what human beings develop cannot be quantified economically or
politically. For the development that allows human beings to become free
is nothing less than the fullest development of their humanity. Thus, only
by recognizing the actual processes by which individuals shape and attach
value to the five freedoms can we understand the development and
progress of human beings who are positioned differently in society (and
frequently in ways that are at variance with their inherited identities and
chosen identifications). Put differently, it is human beings themselves
who must be given the capability space to decide how best to reconcile
these freedoms.

Although Sen thinks that human beings should be afforded that space
individually in the form of progressive developments of capabilities, he
does leave room for three comparisons of different vectors of opportunity
and capability at the level of societies and nation-states. He calls them
total comparison, partial ranking, and distinguished capability comparison;
together, they comprise what Sen calls his direct approach. Total comparison involves "the ranking of all such vectors vis-à-vis each other in

terms of poverty or inequality (or whatever the subject matter is)."[18] Partial ranking involves "the ranking of some vectors vis-à-vis others, but not demanding completeness of the evaluative ranking."[19] Distinguished capability comparison involves "the comparison of some particular capability chosen as the focus, without looking for completeness of coverage."[20] This tripartite scheme is not as hermetically economic as it might sound. Let me offer an example that illustrates both its practical explanatory power and its larger theoretical import outside economics proper. If Sen wants to measure the morbidity rate of women in different parts of the world, he might use the distinguished capability comparison to focus exclusively on women's capability for survival. In this regard, gender is both a necessary and sufficient category of analysis because it can demonstrate different levels of survival for women compared to men, ranging from drastically decreasing to incrementally increasing.

But of course, as Sen himself notes in a 2001 *New Republic* article, "[g]ender inequality is not one homogeneous phenomenon, but a collection of disparate and inter-linked problems. . . . The variations [of gender inequality] entail that inequality between women and men cannot be confronted and overcome by one all-purpose remedy. Over time, moreover, the same country can move from one type of inequality to another."[21] This is why gender inequality cannot just be measured in terms of the deprivation of the ability to survive. Women and men are unequally deprived of many other capabilities and opportunities that, if aggregated, form a complex set of different and even incommensurable inequalities. So while gender is analytically indispensable for analysis of comparative inequality, such analysis as part of the direct approach must deploy the category of gender within total comparison and partial ranking. In other words, gender must be robust enough to analyze and rank order differentials in equality of development not only across a complete vectorial spectrum of capabilities and opportunities, but also within discrete areas of that spectrum (that is, between specific vectors and not others). By analyzing and evaluating vectors this way, gender-based development analysis can significantly strengthen the normative case for expanding women's capabilities. After all, as Sen suggests, "[t]he expansion of women's capabilities not only enhances women's own freedom and well-being, it also has many other effects on the lives of all. An enhancement of women's active agency can contribute substantially to the lives of men as well as women, children as well as adults . . . the greater empowerment of women tends to reduce child neglect and mortality, to decrease fertility and overcrowding, and more generally to broaden social concern and care."[22]

Thinking about development as enhancing the agency and power of women certainly marks Sen's decisive shift from a primary focus on well-being and human flourishing (largely Aristotelian goals) to freedom and agency (largely Kantian and Marxian goals). This thinking also informs what I would call his deeply ethical commitment to feminist theory and practice. Sen wants to say that women's agency increases not only their capability space (and hence their access to the five instrumental freedoms), but also their chance to become political and economic actors and, in the process, promote greater freedom and agency for all. Moreover, women's agency makes possible critical thinking and reflection on the means and end of development within given societies and cultures. "[W]hat is needed is not just freedom of action," Sen therefore claims, "but also freedom of thought—the freedom to question and to scrutinize inherited beliefs and traditional priorities. Informed critical agency is important in combating inequality of every kind, and gender inequality is no exception."[23] Focusing on women's potential freedom and equality with men treats women as free critical agents who do not have to remain trapped by the worst political and economic beliefs, traditions, and practices of patriarchal society. Sen's respect for women as participants in the process of development, as actresses on the stage of history, is but an extension of his understanding of what it means to be fully human—to have the chance to live a life free of hierarchy, domination, and exclusion.

This, precisely, is the understanding that compels him to think of development as both a process and as substantive freedom. Because participation in the process and freedom of development is very much at the heart of Sen's recent thinking, his capabilities approach to development must be thought translatable into an open array of non-teleological economic and political programs at the local, national, and even transnational level. Yet despite this openness within his approach, Sen nonetheless wants to offer a certain perspective on development and indeed on progress. What he vehemently rejects, however, is the idea that such a perspective has anything to do with a linear unfolding of human essence or a strictly teleological path toward development. Wary of the many grand and totalizing theories of development that assert that we can know in advance exactly how humans should develop, Sen concerns himself instead with equalizing the unevenness of global development.

Alongside the direct approach, Sen introduces two other approaches: the supplementary approach and the indirect approach. These three approaches, when combined, comprise the overall economic trajectory of Sen's capabilities approach to development. The supplementary approach starts with traditional procedures for examining income spaces, but then considers capabilities. As Sen states, it "may focus either on direct comparisons of functionings themselves, or on instrumental variables other than income that are expected to influence the determination of capabilities."[24] Either way, this has the effect of extending the informational base on which the income space is measured. On Sen's account, "[s]uch extensions can enrich the overall understanding of problems of inequality and poverty by adding to what gets known through measures of income inequality and income poverty."[25] The indirect approach also focuses on income spaces. But more ambitiously than the supplementary approach, it adjusts income levels by looking at factors besides income that determine capabilities. Here, Sen's core idea is that he can use non-income determinants of capabilities to show whether income is equally distributed within a particular family or familial arrangement. Thus, he argues that "family income levels may be adjusted downward by illiteracy and upward by high levels of education, and so on, to make them equivalent in terms of capability achievement."[26]

The potential flexibility of income adjustment as a means of equalizing the level and number of capabilities achieved reflects Sen's attachment to freedom. This attachment to freedom, which includes an individual's capability to achieve alternate combinations of functioning, leads Sen to think that, in certain development analyses, "the real value of a set of options lies in the best use that can be made of them, and . . . the use that is actually made. . . . In this case, the focusing on a chosen functioning vector coincides with concentration on the capability set, since the latter is judged ultimately by the former."[27] But of course in different circumstances, a particular functioning vector does not always coincide with the concentration on the capability set. This begs the question about the translation of capabilities into functionings. If we contrast a person's capabilities (which include the values that are attributed by different people in different circumstances to specific capabilities) with her ability to translate them into feasible functionings, we can create critical space in which to evaluate and analyze the developmental status of someone whose capabilities cannot be translated into functionings.

There is an ideal aspect to the capabilities approach that leads Sen to break with the traditional economic idea that the value of any chosen set, such as opportunities, is inevitably identified with the best or chosen element of it. As early as the 1970s, in his work on equality of well-being, Sen arguably began to grasp the ideality of the process through which outcomes are generated. Given his recent emphasis on freedom and process, there must be space left open for the generation of outcomes that are not chosen in advance or considered the best. Both this freedom and process, after all, are identified with people actually giving value to the capabilities and functionings they seek. Hence Sen's claim that "[h]aving the option of eating makes fasting what it is . . . choosing not to eat when one could have eaten."[28] In a way, he seems to open up the possibility of approximating a discrete set of capabilities that allows human beings to function in such a way that satisfies basic needs. Sen deliberately refrains, however, from moving in that direction in his latest books—*Development as Freedom* and *Rationality and Freedom*. Rather, he suggests that the democratic construction of needs as a social choice exercise undertaken by political entities ranging from local cooperatives to NGOs to nation-states can serve the freedom that must always remain the means and end of development. On the one hand, he wants to maintain the ideality of capabilities, sometimes tethering this ideality to Adam Smith's impartial spectator, an idealized figure not immediately involved in the conflict at hand, other times tethering it to some other hypothetical experiment in the imagination (for example, Rawls' veil of ignorance) that could guide us, at least on the very abstract and general level, in formulating certain principles by which to index our social choices in institutional and organizational arrangements. On the other hand, he wants to maintain the absolute centrality of political struggle in the articulation of any such ideality. Indeed, Sen has made it clear that freedom and actual democratic struggle must be at the heart of any attempt to translate the capabilities approach and, with it, the five instrumental freedoms, into an institutional or organizational arrangement. Such attempts at translation thus cannot presume that certain people value certain capabilities and functionings over and against others. The space and capability for evaluation must instead be that imputed to people across cultures. This imputation is itself an ideal Kant would have associated with the ideal of humanity. In their ideality, human beings give value both to the world and to themselves; they can transform a world whose conditions they inherited but neither created nor chose.

Sen's insistence on freedom and process can also be found in his approaches to cultural conflict and universal ideals such as freedom. This is particularly striking in his account of how to resolve disputes between different cultures and values, including those concerning religious values and ethnic identifications. Like many political philosophers and anthropologists, Sen observes that cultures are never monolithic in nature because there are always voices of contestation within them—voices powerful enough to divide and transform cultures from within. He goes on, however, to argue that such an observation is not enough to determine how we judge traditions and cultures different from our own. We must defend that space of freedom and contest over the meaning of tradition and cultural authority as integral to every culture's development as freedom. As Sen claims, "There is an inescapable valuational problem involved in deciding what to choose if and when it turns out that some parts of tradition cannot be maintained, along with economic or social changes that may be needed for other reasons. It is a choice that the people involved have to face and assess. . . . If a traditional way of life has to be sacrificed to escape grinding poverty or miniscule longevity . . . then it is the people directly involved who must have the opportunity to participate in deciding what should be chosen. The real conflict is between . . . the basic value that the people must be allowed to decide freely what traditions they wish or [do] not wish to follow; and . . . the insistence that established traditions be followed . . . or, alternatively, people must obey the decisions by religious or secular authorities who enforce traditions—real or imagined."[29]

We can now begin to see how Sen's understanding of the capabilities approach differs from that offered by Martha Nussbaum. In her defense of the capabilities approach, Nussbaum develops a list of capabilities that could be used within nation-states and throughout the world to define those capabilities that must be protected if human beings are to live a truly human life. Following her own reading of Kant, Aristotle, and Marx, Nussbaum foregrounds practical reason in her list of capabilities in such a way that seemingly echoes Immanuel Kant: the capabilities themselves are ethically derived from the dignity of the person. "This idea of human dignity," she argues in *Women and Human Development*, "has broad cross-cultural resonance and intuitive power. . . . I am . . . interested in . . . the level at which a person's capability becomes what Marx called 'truly human,' that is, worthy of a human being. Marx was departing from Kant in some important respects, by stressing (along with Aristotle) that the major powers of a human being need material support and cannot be what they are without it. But he also learned from Kant, and his way of expressing his Aristotelian heritage is distinctively shaped by the Kantian notion of the inviolability and dignity of the person."[30]

The problem attendant upon Nussbaum's attempt to make the capabilities approach the basis for human rights is that she links her conception of equality of well-being to a view of true human functioning. Nussbaum turns to Marx to support the idea that there is something called the truly human, and that there are forms of life that follow from a teleological account of the truly human. She assumes that Marx shares her Kantian conception of the inviolability and dignity of the person. Without getting into all the details of Marx's own relationship to ideals, I want to suggest that Marx was certainly influenced by Kant's conception of how history works behind our backs. In Marx's famous account from *The German Ideology*, what we may think of as truly human is itself only an ideologically imposed view of whatever a particular ruling class takes to be human at any given time. Of course, he certainly argued that freedom must include material freedom to actualize something like our capability to be free. But his communist ideal departs completely from the Aristotelian account of human nature: it imagines a level of diversity and freedom unknown to us in any class society. "From each according to his ability, from each according to his needs": this statement from the

Communist Manifesto is perhaps the most radical, non-liberal conception of distributive justice yet to be dreamt.

Although I am critical of Nussbaum's invocation of Marx as an ally, I think that Marx is indispensable for thinking the ideal of humanity and radicalizing the understanding of distributive justice found in Sen. In his recognition of the institutional freedom of economic facilities, Sen can be pushed from the left to embrace a central Marxist insight: a truly agent-centered conception of development as freedom cannot rely on delivery packages of goods and services; nor can it rely on the idea that distribution to individuals is at the heart of justice. After all, for Marx, workers in a communist society have the capacity not only to control and run their workplaces, but also to confer value on their labor. Thus, the democratic reorganization of production brings democratic contests into the workplace regarding not only how the workplace should be run, but also how work itself should be defined and evaluated. In *Development as Freedom*, Sen recognizes the importance of the establishment of cooperatives for creating jobs and enhancing the value of women's work. Sen accepts certain limits on the market concerning public goods, but he also leaves open the possibility that economic facilities could include certain democratic forms of the reorganization of production and the revaluation of work. In this way, Sen transcends a purely liberal conception of distributive justice. Unlike Sen, Nussbaum wants to hold onto a much more traditional liberal conception of distributive justice involving the distribution of certain discrete and idealized capability sets. My dispute with Nussbaum is not over the value of Sen's capabilities approach as she understands it. Rather, it concerns her attempt to link the ideality of capabilities to a conception of true human functioning that reduces the ideal of humanity to actually existing and limits forms of human life and thereby undercuts the freedom the ideal seeks to promote. For me, this freedom is inseparable from the transnational development of certain regulative ideals and their translation into a program of human rights that nation-states around the world could agree to accept as part of an overlapping consensus.

I want to look more deeply now at Nussbaum's engagement with Sen's understanding of the relationship between functioning and capabilities. Sen, after all, is the one who developed the idea that we need both freedom and equality in order to account for the full diversity of human beings. Sen carefully distinguishes functionings as actual achievements from objectives such as self-respect and the ability to participate in work and other social processes. He always insists that we must distinguish between actual achievement—what we manage to accomplish—and capabilities, which focus on the extent of achievement and the freedom to achieve. He puts the point succinctly in *Inequality Reexamined*: "A person's position in a social arrangement can be judged in two different perspectives . . . (1) the actual achievement and (2) the freedom to achieve. Achievement is concerned with what we manage to accomplish, and freedom with the real opportunity that we have to accomplish what we value."[31] Because Sen is not advocating any standardized form of life for human beings, he has no intention of developing a connection between capabilities and grand universalism, as Nussbaum does in some of her formulations that defend the capabilities approach from an Aristotelian perspective. But perhaps the biggest difference between Nussbaum and Sen can be found—despite her statements to the contrary—in her need to rest her own understanding of the capabilities approach to a strong notion of true human functioning.

She argues that, without at least some level of functioning, certain forms of behavior are not human because they reduce us to the level of animality. "The core idea [of the capabilities approach]," Nussbaum says, "seems to be that of a human being as a dignified free being who shapes his or her own life, rather than being passively shaped or pushed around by the world as if by a member of a 'flock' or 'herd'."[32] Here I want to follow Jane Flax's eloquent critique of Nussbaum's teleological moralism. For Flax, "Nussbaum assumes that human capacities bring with them a moral weight and an obligation for fulfillment within a good life. Identifying what is shared or enumerating our deepest commitments will necessarily lead to a normative idea of human functioning [and human] nature. However, without prior supporting assumptions about its innate qualities, human nature cannot itself be a moral notion. . . . If human nature means 'the way we are'—but this is not already moralized—it might provide a basis for moral judgments. To be plausible, this requires an implicit teleology in which nature, purpose, end, and good are intertwined. Understanding the nature of a thing tells us its purpose and its good. However, Nussbaum does not provide a convincing argument for this teleology. Without it, the moral force of constructing a narrative of a general notion of a human life is lost."[33] Flax goes on to claim, quite rightly, that Nussbaum assumes in her list of capabilities a viewpoint that hierarchizes certain ways of belonging in society and practical reason as the only means of making valuable choices and decisions. This is the problem of trying to derive from a description of human functioning a discrete list of capabilities that enables the evaluation of the lives of individuals. Whenever we start speaking about what is truly human, we necessarily have to say that some of us are more human than others. Moreover, we must demand that those who do not live up to what we see as truly human have lost their dignity and are therefore no longer within the reach of humanity. But because it possesses an irreducible ideality, dignity is something we can never lose. Because of the dignity of a starving woman, we must confront her starvation as that of another human being. If starvation could bring this woman below the level of humanity, as undignified, or worse yet, animal-like, then we might pity her, or try to help her, but we would not be doing so in accordance with the respect her dignity demands.

In her most recent work, Nussbaum explicitly defended an Aristotelian notion of dignity, which she believes can take us beyond Kantian dualism that bases our freedom in our moral reason and relegates our bodily selves with all their complex desires to the realm of the phenomenal. Dignity remains connected to human beings' practical reason, even under Nussbaum's formulation. But it is our complex and "animal selves" that now warrants our respect. This is clearly an attempt, in my mind, to answer critics like Flax who argue that designating even a minimal notion of true human functioning is what gives moral content to the list of capabilities. Nussbaum is in danger of drawing the exact line of above and below who can count as human. Clearly, she wants to do the opposite, by being more inclusive of the complex self that makes us human, a complex self that includes our inherent sociability, our wants and needs, and our dreams and hopes. Although Sen seems to stop short of defining freedom, I believe his work turns on a simple and elegant idea informed by what is best in the Marxist tradition, that our freedom is the freedom to be differently and thus to change our individual and collective lives and histories. This notion of freedom preserves the connection between freedom and dignity, which is why I believe Sen refers to it as a broad deontology, and yet does not fall prey to a rigorous notion of Kantian dualism. This may seem like a subtle difference, but in the end, it is absolutely crucial to the distinction I am drawing between Sen's emphasis on freedom and Nussbaum's own attempt to defend a list of what equality of well-being actually entails. Thus, my first criticism of Nussbaum hinges on our disagreement over the integral connection between freedom and dignity. My second criticism worries about the political and ethical dangers of turning a list of capabilities into a theoretical basis for human rights.

Nussbaum wants to translate her conception of the capabilities approach—which is to say, her view of true human functioning—into the liberal bedrock of human rights. "[R]ights," she argues, "play an increasingly large role outside the account of what the most important capabilities are. Unlike Sen, who prefers to allow the account of the basic capabilities to remain largely implicit in his statements, I have produced an explicit account of the most central capabilities that should be the goal of public policy. The list is being continuously revised and adjusted in accordance with my methodological commitment to cross-cultural deliberation and criticism. But another source of change has been an increasing determination to bring the list down to earth, so to speak, making the thick conception of the good a little less vague, so that it can do real work guiding public policy. At this point, the aim is to come up with the type of specification of a basic capability that could figure in a constitution or perform, apart from that, a constitutional guarantee. In the process, I have increasingly used the language of rights, or the related language of freedom and liberty, in fleshing out the account of capabilities."[34] To her credit, Nussbaum is determined to define this list of capabilities in such a way that it can be sensitive to cultural difference. Indeed, echoing Sen, she claims that "[c]ultures are dynamic and change is a very basic element of them. Contrasts between Western and non-Western societies often depict Western cultures as dynamic, critical, modernizing, while Eastern cultures are identified with oldest elements, as if these do not change or encounter contestation."[35] Unlike Sen or Kant, however, Nussbaum, certainly in her recent writings, tries to justify her capabilities approach on a purely political basis, untying it from her former Aristotelian defense of it. Both Sen and Kant, on the other hand, ultimately take us back to the idea of freedom and in Sen's case, freedom is the value that ultimately justifies the capabilities approach. Although she relies on the dignity of the person and its attachment to the value-making capacity of practical reason, she insists that both the ideal of the person and her list of capabilities are free-standing in John Rawls' sense, meaning that people from many different general and comprehensive world views can develop an overlapping consensus concerning their importance.

Her argument against those who criticize any search for universal values is similar to what she has to say about culture. In her account of the argument for diversity as such—which is the argument against the pursuit of universal values—Nussbaum recognizes the fear that certain U.S. values may be masquerading as universal values. She observes that the argument "from the *good of diversity* reminds us that our world is rich in part because we don't agree on a single set of categories, but speak many different languages of value. Just as we think the world's different languages have worth and beauty, and that it's a bad thing, diminishing the expressive resources of human life generally, when any language ceases to exist, so too we may think that each cultural system has a distinctive beauty, and that it would be an impoverished world if everyone took on the value system of America. Here we must be careful to distinguish two claims the objector might be making. She might be claiming that diversity is good as such; or she might simply be saying that there are problems with the value system of America, and that it would be too bad if the rest of the world emulated our materialism and aggressiveness. The second claim, of course, doesn't yet say anything against universal values, it just suggests that their content should be critical of some American values."[36]

As Nussbaum suggests, what she mainly wants to do with Sen's capabilities approach is bring it down to earth. But if we are not to embrace an avatar of moral or cultural particularism that could actually work to obstruct a defense of human rights, then we must practice Rawls' conjectural reasoning as an ethical corrective to Nussbaum's conception of human rights. Rawls argues that human rights "do not depend on any particular comprehensive moral doctrine or philosophical conception of human nature, such as, for example, that human beings are moral persons and have equal worth, or that they have certain particular moral and intellectual powers that would entitle them to these rights. This would require a quite deep philosophical theory that many, if not most, hierarchical societies might reject as liberal or democratic or in some way distinctive of the Western political tradition and prejudicial to other cultures."[37] When Nussbaum insists on her list of capabilities, she fails to be true to the universality to which she is appealing, because the only way we can reach universality when it comes to human rights is through the conjecture of respect for other conceptions of justice. The real challenge to Nussbaum, then, comes from the ethical demand universality issues to us whenever we participate in discussions about human rights. We may think we understand what we are doing when we make the conjecture of respect for other peoples—for example, that we are heeding the Kantian value of respect. But we should not demand that human rights be tailored strictly on that basis. In my view, practicing this difficult conjectural reasoning is the only way to circumvent the ethical impasse of particularistic conceptions of human rights.

Within the transnational context of a law of peoples, Rawls thinks we can respect different conceptions of justice while at the same time respecting human rights. Despite her arguments to the contrary, Nussbaum ultimately reinscribes liberal universalism as the basis for human rights. Nussbaum does not leave adequate room for the kind of active respect that not only acknowledges as legitimate other conceptions of justice, but also entertains the possibility that there can be an overlapping consensus of divergent theories of justice. Her problem, then, is not that she embraces paternalism, because she does have a defense of that charge. "The argument from paternalism," she argues, "indicates . . . that we should prefer a universal normative account that allows people plenty of liberty to pursue their conceptions of value, within limits set by the protection of the equal worth of the liberties of others. It gives us no good reason to reject all universal accounts, and some strong reasons to construct one, including in our account not only the liberties themselves, but also forms of economic empowerment that are crucial to making those liberties truly available. The argument suggests one more thing: that the account we search for should preserve liberties and opportunities for each and every person, taken one by one, respecting each of them as an end, rather than simply as the agent or the supporter of the ends of others."[38] The problem that she does not see is exactly the one Rawls so clearly articulates. Her very idea of the person, here, implies an acceptance of a certain variant of liberalism as a general and comprehensive world-view, in Rawls' sense. Ultimately then, she cannot, as she seeks to do, defend her capabilities list as free-standing. In this sense, then, in her answer to paternalism, she embraces a liberalism that would encapture human rights in one general and comprehensive world-view that would necessarily exclude others, and by so doing, would fail the attempt to make norms universalizable. My debate with Nussbaum, then, turns on an ethical concern about how universality should be achieved in human rights discourses, and not on the other charges that have been made against her, such as the importance of cultural relativism and diversity, or the dangers of paternalism.

Although Sen seems to recoil from liberal universalism as a general and comprehensive world-view, he nonetheless embraces a certain spirit of it in the name of the universal ideal of freedom. "Grand universalism," he argues in his 2002 essay "Justice Across Borders," "has an ethical stature that draws on its comprehensive coverage and nonsectarian openness. It rivals the universalism of classical utilitarianism and that of a generalized interpretation of the Kantian conception of reasoned ethics. It can speak in the name of the whole of humanity in a way that the separatism of national particularist conceptions would not allow."[39] Sen agrees with me that Rawls attempted to develop his law of peoples by applying the original position to international relations between nation-states because he wanted to expand the reach of tolerance and respect to all societies, thereby avoiding the imposition of Western liberalism as the only general and comprehensive world-view. Sen's concern, however, is that this attempt ties us into our national identities in such a way that undermines our actual freedom to express ourselves in multiple identifications and affiliations. In Sen's view, this focus on international relations simply does not capture the multiple affiliations, organizations, and agencies already operative in many struggles to achieve global justice. "Requirements of global justice," he claims, "offer guidance in diverse voices and sometimes in conflicting directions. Although we cannot escape the need for critical scrutiny of the respective demands, this is not a reason for expecting to find one canonical superdevice that will readily resolve all the diversities of obligations that relate to our various affiliations, identities, and priorities. The oversimplification that must be particularly avoided is to identify global justice with international justice. The reach and relevance of the former can far exceed those of the latter."[40] Sen's concern with oversimplification takes us back to the central place he accords freedom, including the freedom to democratically contest the meaning of global justice itself. Thus, our ability to exceed any one identity for ourselves is crucial to how we emphasize freedom in our efforts to achieve social justice.

If we interpret our multiple political affiliations, identities, and priorities as embattled configurations of the ideal of humanity, as Sen himself sometimes seem to understand them, then Sen's appeal to universality and his conception of this political multiplicity are rather close to Étienne Balibar's fictive universality and his understanding of civility as a regulative ideal that helps us grapple with the affiliations and organizations we seek to develop in order to achieve transnational justice. Sen himself uses the phrase "global justice," but a careful reading of his descriptions of how organizations and institutions develop our affiliations signals his interest in something closer to transnational justice. Indeed, Sen focuses on actual organizational efforts that are not international in Rawls' sense, but rather transnational in the sense that nationality and ethnicity do not exclusively ground them. Thus, he suggests that "[t]he starting point for an alternative approach, drawing on plural affiliations, can be the recognition of the fact that we all have multiple identities, and that each of these identities can yield concerns and demands that can significantly supplement, or seriously compete with, other concerns and demands arising from other identities."[41] But as Balibar explains, fictive universality is promoted by institutions that allow us not only to have complex identities, but also to undergo processes of individualization in which we make sense of the social and political relations that determine our various identities. Where Balibar and Sen converge here is in their insistence that these institutions should be defended precisely because they promote freedom.

Reading Sen through the lens of Balibar, Sen's definition of freedom as capability space and the five instrumental freedoms that expand that space can be considered fictive not because they are unreal but because, through their ethical and political desirability, we are endlessly promoting them and bringing them into being. If freedom includes the freedom to be different as well as the freedom to give value to our lives, there must be a fictive dimension to it, because we inevitably determine and represent what counts as freedom in every institutionalization of it. Sen defends a critical notion of the ideal of humanity—critical in the sense that it is a negative limit against any claims concerning a particular form of humanity being the ultimate form of what we are and what we can become as human beings. The appeal to the ideal of humanity enables us to critique nationalist particularism and other exclusionary forms of political organization. Thus, Sen claims that "even the identity of being a human being—perhaps our most basic identity—may have the effect, when fully seized, of broadening our viewpoint, and the imperatives that we may associate with our shared humanity may not be mediated by our membership in collectivities such as 'nations' or 'peoples'."[42]

This broadening of viewpoint through the ideal of humanity as a critical force opens up the space for the ideal of civility. Balibar's notion of civility turns on his assessment of the limits and strengths of fictive universality. On Balibar's account, fictive universality follows from Hegel's idea that every society and nation-state develops norms, institutional structures, and ways of life that circumscribe the political entitlement to subjectivity and hence who within the political realm can be recognized as a subject. National ideals coupled with moral expressions of the ideal of humanity animate this fictive universality. And struggles within fictive universality inevitably involve struggles for political recognition and the expansion of politically recognizable subjectivity. This is why Balibar understands the need to defend universality as a symbol, which is transnational by definition because it carries something beyond itself—an appeal that it is an insurrection against the limits of universality as defined by the modern nation-state and the forms of political subjectivity it is willing to recognize. Fictive and symbolic universality, when brought together, advance Balibar's ideal of civility as a regulative ideal. Pitting Hegel against Hegel, as it were, Balibar wants to radicalize Hegel's politicization of subjectivity by rejecting the straight-laced Hegelian conception of progress in which stages of human development are necessarily reflected in the institutional arrangements and structures of the modern nation-state.

What Balibar finds normatively desirable in Hegel's political philosophy are internal processes of individualization supported by national and in some cases transnational associations and other forms of institutional structures. As he argues, "[t]he true universalistic element, however, lies in the *internal* process of individualization: virtual deconstruction and reconstruction of primary identities. And it is all the more effective when it has been achieved through difficult and violent conflicts, where oppression and revolt have threatened the hegemonic structure with internal collapse. 'Individualized individuals' . . . are created through the conflictual (dis)integration of primary memberships—that is to say, when individuals can view the wider community as a *liberating* agency, which frees them from belonging to one single group, or possessing a single, undifferentiated, massive identity. It is universalistic because . . . it is working both *from above* and *from below* with respect to 'particular' groups and communities."[43] The process of deconstructive and reconstructive identity formation allows not only complex relations between particular groups and communities, but also space for transnational political relations and forms of organization. In this way, Balibar conceives a political form of universality irreducible to Nussbaum's liberal universalism.

Rather deftly, he suggests that the forms of multiculturalism associated with fictive universality have often been much more advanced in parts of the world typically considered "underdeveloped" and indeed challenge us to think of new cultural and political forms that may be modern but in diverse and truly multiple ways. On his account, the phenomenon of transnational migrations "acquires a new quality. It is here, particularly, that a precise historical analysis is required in order to avoid simplistic 'Eurocentric' or 'Western' prejudices . . . [C]olonial and 'Third World' countries have long experienced what we in the 'North' now call *multiculturalism*. Far from being 'backward' in this respect, they were showing the way. It becomes clear that this highly conflictual and also evolutionary pattern was not a transitory one . . . Whether or not this will be compatible with the simple continuation of the political and cultural forms which had emerged with European (and North American) hegemony, notably the (more or less completely sovereign) nation-state and (more or less unified) national culture, is exactly what is at stake in current debates on 'the New World Order', on dominant and dominated languages, religious and literary standards in education, and so on."[44]

For Balibar, civility is a politics that "regulates the conflict of identifications between the impossible (and yet, in a sense, very real) limits of a total and floating identification, 'civility'. Civility in this sense is certainly not a politics which suppresses all violence; but it excludes extremes of violence, so as to *create a* (public, private) *space* for politics (emancipation, transformation), and enable violence itself to be historicized."[45] In a sense, this ideal approximates Sen's fairness as arbitration because it emphasizes the creation of public space for both self-reflection and debate. But I find the ideal of civility more normatively desirable, although the aspect of fairness in Sen means that we can imagine ourselves both inside and outside our complex identities and positions—both nationally and otherwise—because we actually have institutional structures that promote us in doing just that. Nevertheless, Sen can be understood to argue that transnational institutions and agencies are actually creating and reinforcing the kind of space which, by allowing complex identities and positions as well as enhancing freedom, also promotes civility as a political ideal. Although it certainly appeals to the symbolic universality of the ideal of humanity, this political ideal is not empty in Sen; it has institutional support. Properly imputed to Sen's account of fairness and arbitration, the ideality of civility can guide us further in envisioning our political positions, identities, and identifications, for it allows us to imagine ourselves as connected to various peoples and identities and thus to struggle for peace and justice. Civility, then, is regulative; it is suffused by institutions and norms, but it also enables us to critique forms of aggressive national and ethnic identity without at the same time denying the cultures and ethnicities with which we identify, and the states and nations that position us. Civility is the political ideal by which we understand our relation to those identifications and positions that inform our engagements and conflicts with others—engagements and conflicts that arise in the dramatic global form of threats of war but also in local forms of political contestation concerning border negotiations and the recognition of certain human rights. It is this civility that can promote what Sen describes as fair arbitration between complex organizational structures. As a regulative ideal, we project it into the future as if it were a real guide; it is not a goal to be achieved, but rather an ideal that directs our political struggles for emancipation and transformation.

Civilization, Progress, and Beyond 5

In 1962, the German political philosopher Theodor W. Adorno memorably wrote that "[l]ike every philosophical term, 'progress' has its equivocations; and as in any such term, these equivocations also register a commonality. What at this time should be understood by the term 'progress' one knows vaguely, but precisely: for just this reason one cannot apply the concept roughly enough. To use the term pedantically merely cheats it out of what it promises: an answer to the doubt and the hope that things will finally get better, that people will at last be able to breathe a sigh of relief."[1] Certainly it is impossible to breathe such a sigh of relief in these terrible times. Shortly after September 11, the United States declared that "we" were at war with the "axis of evil," including but hardly excluded to Al-Qaeda. Since then, "we" have bombed Afghanistan and conquered Iraq. I put "we" in quotation marks because I was one of the hundreds of thousands who marched and protested week after week, month after month, with the hope that war could be avoided. There was reason to hope, after all, because the UN's weapons inspectors dutifully reported that Iraq did not pose a national security threat to the United States. But facts have not mattered much to the Bush administration. And "we" are not to be bothered by them either. Anyone who boorishly insists on facts is un-American and reminded that "we" are at war. Bush has declared that the war against Iraq is now officially over but not the real war. The other one. The big one. The infinite war on terror. Iraq is just one battlefield, and in that battlefield, the war is clearly not over. How can anyone breathe a sigh of relief when the battles in Iraq continue to intensify and we are told there soon will be other battlefields? It has never been more difficult to believe in the ideal of progress—an ideal whose history is not that pretty, bound up as it is with imperialism and war.

If we think, as some conservative game theorists do, merely in terms of nation-states attacking each other *ad infinitum* until they reach a military endgame, we obscure all too easily the massive human suffering and deaths that war always leaves in its wake. Under the cloud of catastrophe, we would do well to remember that the ongoing threat of a nuclear disaster in which the death toll reaches mathematically sublime proportions has actually been looming over us ever since the United States dropped two atomic bombs on Japan, bringing hell to earth for more than a million people. But the Bush administration would rather dispense with the tepid taboo on the use of nuclear weapons and reclaim the potential military importance of weapons of mass destruction for U.S. foreign relations.

Recently, Étienne Balibar has distinguished cruelty from *Gewalt* or more traditional forms of violence, including what we think of as the lawful violence of the judicial system and the enforcement mechanisms of the modern state. For him, cruelty and violence have different relationships to ideality, including the great ideals of freedom and equality and the movement in the direction of those ideals; in other words, progress. Balibar argues that "the violence-of-power, the *Gewalt*, has an immediate relationship with historical ideality and idealities, because, while it serves some very precise public and private interests, it never ceases to embody idealities, to implement them, to constitute itself as the force which crushes all resistance in order to embody idealities or ideal principles: God, the Nation, the Market . . . The forms of cruelty, on the other hand, have a relationship with materiality which is not mediated (especially not symbolically mediated), although in this immediate relationship with materiality some terrible idealities return, so to speak, or become displayed and exhibited as fetishes or emblems."[2] At first glance, Balibar's analysis of *Gewalt* seems to accept, à la Ernesto Laclau, that all forms of ideality are but the result of the struggle for hegemony for those groups that want to impose and legitimate their own ideals as those that should be realized. Laclau, by making an idiosyncratic distinction between the ethical and the normative, renders the struggle for hegemony such that it equalizes all idealities as inevitably normative and therefore conservative. In a recent essay, he argues that "there is no logical transition from an unavoidable ethical moment, in which the fullness of society manifests itself as an empty symbol, to any particular normative order. There is an ethical investment in particular normative orders, but no normative order which is, in and for itself, ethical. . . . Hegemony is, in this sense, the name for this unstable relation between the *ethical* and the *normative*, our way of addressing this infinite process of investments which draws its dignity from its very failure."[3]

In other words, because the causal basis of ideals is the same, there is no determinable basis upon which to distinguish normatively better and worse ideals. This is why Laclau thinks the great ideals are always empty signifiers: they are given symbolic content by the relations of power and violence that dictate the realization of certain ideals over and against others. Unlike Laclau, Balibar not only defends the importance of ideals, but also recognizes that the justifications, articulations, and imaginings of ideals are precisely what mediate them symbolically. His position is thus that political and ethical discourse concerning ideals can occur only at the level of mediation. Hence all the great debates Balibar associates with the tradition of equaliberty: how does one reconcile freedom and equality? If equality tells us who and rights to liberty tell us what, how do we make sense of the who and the what?[4] Can we defend justice within the traditional ideals of freedom and equality? In this way, the ideals of equaliberty have a whole complex set of mediated meanings. And those meanings are irreducible to any causal link to the struggle for hegemony. Balibar's whole point, then, is to distinguish violence that necessitates mediation and discourse from those forms of cruel social relations that put such necessity under erasure.

"You're either with us or against us": in precisely Balibar's sense, this remains the politically and symbolically unmediated response to September 11—the cruel response that tries to deaden discourse and even political action as possible defenses of alternative responses and ideals. All too often those who have stood by the ideal principles most basic to the United States—those embodied in its constitution, including the Congressional check against the authority of the executive branch to use military force as a means of solving international conflicts—have not prevailed. When Barbara Lee, a progressive representative from California, dared to speak out against the U.S. Congress giving President Bush extended war powers in the "infinite war" against terror, she was lambasted and considered un-American. She defended her position by reading from the Constitution. When Robert Byrd, a conservative senator from West Virginia, filibustered through the night to fight against the Homeland Security Act, he too was accused of being un-American. His political act was simply informed by the ideals of the Constitution. He lost and despairingly described himself as "speaking to the ocean."[5] Despite the failures of Lee and Byrd, the political ideals of freedom and justice found in the Constitution and the Bill of Rights continue to be the dominant political ideals that most Americans recognize and claim as their own.

In December 2002, *The New York Times* published an article that suggested that the problem with liberals—including John Rawls, the great philosopher of political liberalism—is their continuing investment in ideal principles as the only legitimate basis for security and stability. Rawls is chided for not knowing how to handle the bullies on the playground (i.e., the terrorists). Military force—not ideals—is seen as the only way we can "effectively" deal with terrorists.[6] But progressive idealists in the global anti-war movement are with Rawls in insisting on the mediation of violence by ideals and are thus pitting themselves against what Balibar identifies as cruelty; the cruelty that treats the citizens of Iraq as disposable people. Put more strongly, if we do not defend ideals and, following Balibar, distinguish between violence and cruelty, then we will not be able to challenge the current war mongering of the Bush administration.

Some might rejoin here that Bush himself has appealed to ideals; after all, the war in Iraq was renamed "Operation Iraqi Freedom." The response to this rejoinder from the movement for peace and justice should be that Bush's appeals have been to fetishes and emblems, not to ideals as such, because his appeals work to divest ideals of any significant ideational and symbolic content. In his speeches, Bush does not defend the curtailment of civil liberties and civil rights for a counter-ideal of security because he does not seek to reason with us at all. Instead, he uplifts the United States as the vigilant watchdog of the world whose military action must proceed if the citizens of the United States are to be safe. The difficult job of the Left is then to defend ideals in the exact opposite way so as to promote public discussion and democratic forums for how we should respond to terrorism. Progress demands that we see the Bush administration's cruelty for what it is.

In the fall of 2002, I helped form a social justice organization in New York City called Take Back the Future. Ann Snitow, long-time feminist activist and professor of literature at New School University, shared the main organizational effort and vision with me. We chose the name both for its feminist resonance with Take Back the Night and because we believe that the future of constitutional democracy and of "civilized" humanity are at stake. As a group, we want to struggle for a better political and ethical future. In our view, we can only achieve such a future by returning to the ideal of humanity, which forces us to grapple with two of the most notorious political ideals of Western modernity—progress and civilization. Indeed, although members of the group have many different philosophical backgrounds and political affiliations, we all share a commitment to ideals and ideality in Balibar's sense. We are therefore, unabashedly, idealists. We think we need to return the Left to a mediated struggle about which ideals are worth defending now and how we should go about defending them. If there is a basis of unity in our agreement, it is not that we necessarily agree on the same ideals, but that we believe that the Left must return to the battle over ideals and attack the cruelty of the Bush administration. We believe this can take place only by defending the complexity of our current situation and yet showing that a defense of ideals and ideality is still possible. We have already done this on the level of practice. As a direct action group that has tried to take the message of peace and constitutional rights and democracy to the streets, we have marched without a police permit in the name of the First Amendment to the Constitution, which guarantees citizens of the United States freedom of speech. Moreover, we have defended the free exercise of religion in support of the Muslim community when Muslim residents, legally living in this country, were forced to undergo a humiliating practice of registering with the INS[7] by January 10, 2003, for no other reason than they were from certain allegedly suspect countries in the Arab world.

What has happened to the Muslim community in New York City and throughout the United States forces us to reconsider some of our most controversial ideals, including civilization and progress, especially since writers such as Bernard Lewis and Samuel Huntington have increasingly accused the Muslim world of being monolithic and provincial. It has thus never been more important to think about how we conceive of progress and civilization, precisely because both ideals have become inextricably linked in recent political discourse. To speak of securing the future is to speak of progress. This simple proposition is not politically unpalatable or unthinkable for many intellectuals. After all, it is certainly in keeping with the thinking of someone like Richard Rorty, who argues that the United States and other modern Western democracies represent a kind of progress that should make us proud and that we should celebrate through patriotism. Rorty hails the technological advancements not just of the United States in particular, but of humankind in general.[8] To be sure, many hard-nosed conservative intellectuals and pundits would disagree with Rorty's sunny view of progress—a view that seems to imply that we cannot but continue progressing, even if there is some back-sliding along the way. These conservatives tend to be positivists who think that we must be prepared to eliminate the eliminator, no matter what the cost.

However, as Adorno suggests in his essay on progress, this position quickly reduces to the idea that "radical evil legitimates evil."[9] "This conviction," he argues, "wields a catchphrase with which it obscurantistically condemns progress in modern times: the belief in progress. The attitude of those who defame the concept of progress as insipid and positivistic is usually positivistic itself. They explain the way of the world, which repeatedly thwarted progress and which also always was progress, as evidence that the world plan does not tolerate progress and that whoever does not renounce it commits sacrilege. In self-righteous profundity one takes the side of the terrible, slandering the idea of progress according to the schema that whatever human beings fail at is ontologically refused them, and that in the name of their finitude and mortality they have the duty to wholeheartedly appropriate both of these qualities. A sober response to this false reverence would be that while indeed progress from the slingshot to the megaton bomb may well amount to satanic laughter, in the age of the bomb a condition can be envisaged for the first time in which violence might vanish altogether."[10]

Enlisting Adorno as an ally in the defense of ideals may seem surprising because Adorno is often thought of as a critic of idealism, particularly of the Kantian variety. Before we address some aspects of Adorno's relationship to Kant, let us consider Jay Bernstein's succinct description of Adorno's understanding of the relationship between the civilization of self-preservation and the civilization of humanity. The first kind of civilization, defended by Hobbes, is inseparable from the reduction of moral categories to the balancing of appetites and aversions and ultimately the desire to escape from death; the second, defended by Kant, is inseparable from the priceless worth of every human being and the ideal of humanity. According to Bernstein, "Adorno reads civilization, the long history of human socialization, as a fragile synthesis of civilization as self-preservation and civilization as humanity, as answerable both to instrumental and non-instrumental ends, as providing a response to the need for order and cooperation, on the one hand, and to a moral conception of human worth and dignity on the other. This fragile synthesis comes under siege in modernity when what was a synthesis comes to be interpreted in terms of the civilization of humanity (the unconditioned end) becoming the instrument for the realization of humanity as self-preservation."[11]

On Adorno's account, instrumental rationality legitimates the idea of self-preservation—the idea that human beings found a nation-state because, without a sovereign to preserve their life and provide for their security, they are left only with their murderous instincts and hence the constant threat of death. Moreover, for Adorno, this understanding of the social contract (elaborated, of course, in full detail by Hobbes) is inseparable from the disenchantment of the modern world in which domination over nature becomes the sign of progress as human beings develop ever greater techniques and skills to ensure that man rules the world. The great irony, however, is that these techniques and skills are precisely what prevent the idea of self-preservation—the mere protection of bare life, the simple survival of human beings—from being a politically sustainable reality. Indeed, the great technological advancements produced by Western modernity have enabled human beings to destroy the ozone layer and deplete the world's natural resources at the same time that they have become part of the dynamics of war and advanced capitalism. For Adorno, the very idea of self-preservation and the progress associated with the civilization it produces do not value humanity except insofar as human beings further the relentless march of skill and technique—a death-march in which human progress is measured with the blood and toil of human suffering. The ideal of humanity reduces, then, to the onslaught of man against nature and the technocratic management of human beings with the ultimate skill and technique—nuclear weapons. Progress can only have meaning if we wrest its concept from the civilization of self-preservation that subsumes itself in the brutish ideal of an already-realized humanity that exploits the supposedly ineluctable reality of human life. "The explosive tendency of progress," Adorno therefore claims, "is not merely the Other to the movement of a progressing domination of nature, not just its abstract negation; rather it requires the unfolding of reason through the very domination of nature. Only reason, the principle of societal domination inverted into the subject, would be capable of abolishing this domination."[12]

Here we encounter Adorno's complex understanding and suspicion of progress such as it follows from the paradox (we might even call it the aporia) of reason found within modern subjectivity itself. "Only those reflections about progress have truth," he says in a related passage, "that immerse themselves in progress and yet maintain distance, withdrawing from paralyzing facts and specialized meanings. Today reflections of this kind come to a point in the contemplation of whether humanity is capable of preventing catastrophe. The forms of humanity's own global societal constitution threaten its life, if a self-conscious global subject does not develop and intervene. The possibility of progress, of averting the most extreme, total disaster, has migrated to this global subject alone."[13] The need for imagining such a global subject requires us to think critically about the attempts of the United States and some of the most powerful countries in Western Europe to constitute the universal future of humanity. Indeed, we must consider what subject is capable of intervening in every region of the world, what this subject looks like, and for whom its globalization is desirable as a political ideal. The dream of a global subject, then, seems hopeless without a world government or confederation of nation-states working together to create and universalize political transformation. It also appears to invite the re-legitimation of empire and imperialism, not to mention the civilizing mission of Victorian liberalism that justified much of modern colonization. Moreover, it can serve as an ideological fodder for those who want to shore up the role of the United States as guarantor of liberty and democracy throughout the world. Assessing the validity of Adorno's clarion call for a global subject demands, then, that we come to grips with the most searing contemporary critiques of universalism without giving up on the ideal of humanity and its power to halt the systematic destruction of human life.

We can only do this if we consider his growing respect for Kant late in life. Adorno, after all, claims that Kant "incorruptibly maintained the unity of reason even in its contradictory uses—the nature-dominating, what he called theoretical, causal-mechanical, and the power of judgment snuggling up to nature in reconciliation—and displaced reason's difference strictly into the self-limitation of nature-dominating reason."[14] His point is that reason's urge to conquer the natural world is limited by reason itself. This self-limitation opens up space for reflection and judgment such that reason can attempt to reconcile itself with the very thing it attempts to dwarf and dominate, namely nature. The dialectical maintenance of reason as both unified and divided allows reconciliation and resistance to domination to remain open as rational possibilities. In this way, Adorno envisages the political and ethical importance of reason achieving neither practical nor theoretical closure. He sees that, through a concept of reconciliation, Kant avoids asserting the simple identity between the belief in unreflective positivism and the ideal of progress.

Reconciliation for Adorno is not a re-found unity of subject and object. Instead, it maintains the antinomy between them and, more precisely, the antinomy between the ideal of humanity remaining other to history and humankind being thoroughly historical. What Adorno emphasizes is that Kant refuses the kind of positivism associated with progress—a positivism that can take two forms: the first is that we can ultimately know all that exists and conquer it, until we exhaust the limits of human life. But of course, the human subject as the ultimate know-it-all is exactly what Kant's view of humankind denies. The second kind of positivism Adorno associates with one reading of Hegel and especially those who fail to grapple with the ethical and political complexity attendant upon *Geist*.[15] On this standard interpretation of Hegel, Hegel defends a normative ideal of human development that is a one-way street to the democratic modernity that the Western democracies have purportedly achieved. Under this Hegelian view, progress is equated with particular social and political forms. We know the list: individual rights, constitutional government, the separation of church and state, etc. This conception of progress turns on an interior unfolding of human essence that we can subjectively grasp and instrumentally rationalize. But what Adorno finds in Kant is a history of humankind and even progress that cannot be fully rationalized because it works behind the backs of human beings.

At his most optimistic, Kant claims that human beings should aspire to the glorious solidarity of the kingdom of ends in which other great ideals such as freedom, equality, and even perpetual peace could be other than mere dreams. He has a certain faith in what human beings and nation-states might achieve in the form of the institutionalization of political ideals—what Balibar calls equaliberty—which could in turn lead to perpetual peace on an international level. But the Kant that Adorno considers an ally is not the optimistic Kant. Adorno's claim that progress must turn on the prevention of catastrophe through the self-limitation and inversion of instrumental reason is reflected in Kant's negative dialectic of unsocial sociability. Kant's thought was basically this: far from humans having the full development of their humanity as their destiny, it may be precisely our unsociability as a ruse of nature that drives us not only to develop cultural and political forms of resistance against instrumental reason, but also to look disaster in the face and seek to escape it. As he wrote in his "Idea for a Universal History," "Nature has thus again employed the unsociableness of men, and even of the large societies and states which human beings construct, as a means of arriving at a condition of calm and security through their inevitable antagonism. Wars, tense and unremitting military preparations, and the resultant distress which every state must eventually feel within itself, even in the midst of peace—these are the means by which nature drives nations to make initially imperfect attempts, but finally, after many devastations, upheavals and even complete inner exhaustion of their powers, to take the step which reason could have suggested to them without so many sad experiences—that of abandoning a lawless state of savagery and entering a federation of peoples in which every state, even the smallest, could expect to derive its security and rights not from its own power or its own legal judgment, but solely from this great federation (*Foedus Amphictyonum*), from a united power and the law-governed decisions of a united will."[16] What Adorno shares with Kant is the view that unsocial sociability undermines the explanations of those who deny progress in the name of reality. Today we hear such explanations endlessly repeated in pseudo-Hegelian theses about how late capitalism has brought an end to history and inaugurated a new world order, thereby proving that there can be no human progress beyond an advanced capitalist world system. Behind this idea of no more progress is a positivistic illusion that a scientific understanding of human nature, the triumph of free market economics, and the institutions necessary to achieve material success within individual nations and throughout the world can be reduced to a set of iron formulas and laws. But both Kant and Adorno agree that, even if human beings were a race of devils, they would nonetheless be able to prevent the fate of their own destruction. This possibility of preventing destruction is at the heart of what Adorno means by progress. Indeed, Adorno analyzes the idea that progress ends with capitalism as an ideological construct of bourgeois society.

"Not until the bourgeois class had occupied the decisive positions of power," Adorno claims, "did the concept of progress degenerate into the ideology that ideological profundity then accused the nineteenth century of harboring. The nineteenth century came up against the limit of bourgeois society, which could not fulfill its own reason, its own ideals of freedom, justice and humane immediacy, without running the risk of its order being abolished. This made it necessary for society to credit itself, untruthfully, with having achieved what it had failed."[17] With regard to the United States, Adorno would no doubt claim that we fail to realize the ideals of freedom, justice, and humane immediacy because they are incompatible with the economic disparity between the wealthy few and everyone else, which is symptomatic of our larger hierarchical control over both natural resources and world markets.

In any case, what Adorno completely rejects is any idea that there is an essence of humanity knowable as truth that unwinds itself in an upward spiral yielding finally the unification of the knowledge of human beings with their spirit and freedom. For Adorno, the shadow of nineteenth-century imperialism is precisely the dark cloud of Hegelian *Geist*, the Western spirit of humanity, dominating the rest of the world such that the modern rational subject achieves a totality in which its various incarnations constitute all that humanity can become. Yet despite Adorno's critical remarks about subjectivity fully rationalized and represented as the conqueror of nature, Adorno is ethically committed to a different, more limited conception of subjectivity he associates with his own idiosyncratically Hegelian conception of modernity. The best way for us to understand Adorno's apprehensive adherence to modern subjectivity is by considering what Balibar has called fictive universality, which is "not the idea that the common nature of individuals is given or already there, but, rather, the fact that it is produced in as much as particular identities are relativized, and become mediations for the realization of a superior and more abstract goal."[18]

Balibar uses the term "fictive" not in any literary sense. Yet he also does so to note that the stage of modernity that Hegel so carefully tried to articulate in his *Philosophy of Right* is one in which human subjectivity is fully unleashed as a force in history such as to allow human beings the space of self-representation. Human beings are freed enough from their determination by hierarchically established positions in society that they can dream of freedom—including their own individuality as a person—and create something of a life not from the abyss of absolute freedom but from the complexity of social roles (roles such as those in the family, professions, classes, etc.) in which individuals are constituted and yet to which they can never be fully reduced. We need to hold onto fictive universality because ethically it allows us not only to recognize the complexity of our identities and identifications, but also to bring onto the stage of history the possibility of re-imagining humanity through coming to grips with that very complexity. While Adorno does not use Balibar's language, he still seeks to make a similar point when he writes of reason reflecting upon itself such that the affirmation of subjectivity over and against substance exceeds the province of theoretical reason, thereby finding its home in a world of praxis in which human beings always transform themselves. "[R]eason would see through itself," Adorno writes, "as a moment of praxis and would recognize, instead of mistaking itself for the absolute, that it is a mode of behavior. The anti-mythological element in progress cannot be conceived without the practical act that reins in the delusion of spirit's autarky. Hence progress can hardly be ascertained by disinterested contemplation."[19] What Adorno wants to say is that it is precisely a complex subject that can achieve some degree of self-reflection and thus thwart the global substance that can be so grandiosely proclaimed as a political essence. Through certain forms of political practice, this subject can challenge its own determination by forces external to it and mobilize actual living human beings against the all-too-real threat of catastrophe.

Is Adorno simply restating Marx's famous declaration that men make their own history but not under conditions of their choosing? Adorno wants to link Marx's conception of historical change and praxis with Kant's complex understanding of reconciliation and antagonism between nature and culture. Indeed, by his reading, "where Kant comes closest to the concept of reconciliation, in the thought that the antagonism terminates in its abolition, appears the catchword of a society in which freedom is 'bound up with irresistible power.' Yet even the talk of progress recalls the dialectic of progress itself. While the perpetual oppression that unleashed progress at the same time always arrested it, this oppression . . . first made the antagonism and the whole extent of the deception recognizable at all, the prerequisite for settling the antagonism. The progress . . . is that finally progress can begin, at any moment."[20]

To summarize Adorno: humankind developing through a drive for self-preservation represents this struggle in the name of the ideal of humanity rather than its mere attempt at survival. Thus, the re-imagining of this grand ideal is linked with the basic drive for survival *and* the space in which universality can be represented differently as the civilization of humanity. With his notion of unsocial sociability, Kant shows us how nature as a great artificer may produce a fairly disastrous work of art: human beings who have only come together in order to preserve themselves, and yet cannot seem to avoid being the bullies on the playground. Kant, of course, did not live to see the mega-ton bomb, but he did live to see enough of the emergence of nation-states to understand that endless war was a real and constant threat. And yet ironically, it was also this threat, and perhaps only this threat, that would serve as a wake-up call to the peoples of the world to commit themselves to the ideal of perpetual peace. This is why Adorno rejects the idea that progress can ever be simplistically identified with a knowable, optimistically described, design of human nature. "The concept of universal history is plausible," Adorno therefore argues, "only as long as one can believe in the illusion of an already existing humanity, coherent in itself and moving upwards as a unity. If humanity remains entrapped by the totality it itself fashions . . . no progress has taken place at all, while mere totality nevertheless allows progress to be entertained in thought. This can be elucidated most simply by the definition of humanity as that which excludes absolutely nothing. If humanity were a totality that no longer held within it any limiting principle, then it would also be free of the coercion that subjects all its members to such a principle and thereby would no longer be a totality: no forced unity."[21]

The critique of totality protects the ideality of humanity by separating any analysis of who we are from who we might become in our aspirations to guide ourselves by reconfigurations of the ideal itself. These imaginings of who we might become demand that we project a future of what might be. Progress lies in the promise of this difference: that we can always transform ourselves as we imagine new forms of social life. If we reduce the future to the present, then we lose sight of progress. In the end, the denial of progress is the denial of the idea that there can ever be a different, and better, future.

How does Kant's conception of the ideal of humanity align with Adorno's projection of a future yet to come that is necessary in any imagining of the ideal? We must emphasize that for Kant the great ideals— including humanity itself—are always regulative rather than constitutive. They regulate human practice as we try to envision, realize, and even critique them. They are formed not in abstract mental space, but in the social and political world that mediates and indeed limits them symbolically. Kant's point here is not reducible to the sociological insight that the ideal of humanity must always be open for social and political contest and that, in this contest, the shape of the ideals will change. "Any high praise for *the ideal of humanity* in its moral perfection," he argues in *The Metaphysics of Morals*, "can lose nothing in practical reality from examples to the contrary, drawn from what human beings now are, have become, or will presumably become in the future. . . ."[22] Of course, Adorno, and more than likely Kant, had he lived to see the new social movements, thinks there will always be new groups that claim themselves as human. As they claim themselves as human, the ideal of humanity shifts its meaning in order to include them.

But humanity as an ideal must be *thought* beyond all given representations even if it can only be brought to earth within them. If humanity could be collapsed into any set of historical symbols or representations, then any group excluded from the same would not be able to re-imagine the ideal differently—certain representations would, as a result, remain hegemonic. That in and of itself would be a bad thing. But Adorno's point runs deeper. The appeal to the universality of humanity carries within it a critique of identity thinking in Adorno's sense, because all configurations of the ideal point beyond themselves to the future of what has yet to be revealed in the current forms of our humanity. Hence, the universality promised by the ideal, which is that it could encompass all that we could ever be through time and space, is always beyond any particular set of symbolizations. As a result, symbolizations of the ideal can always be challenged by other symbolizations and representations. It is Adorno's understanding of how the ideal of humanity necessarily respects multiplicity rather than totality that allows him to reclaim it for critical theory.

But where does that leave progress, and how does the ideal of humanity relate to this understanding? "If progress were truly master of the whole, the concept of which bears the marks of its violence," Adorno writes at the end of his essay on progress, "then progress would no longer be totalitarian. Progress is not a conclusive category. It wants to cut short the triumph of radical evil, not to triumph as such itself. A situation is conceivable in which the category would lose its meaning, and yet which is not the situation of universal regression that allies itself with progress today. In this case, progress would transform itself into the resistance to the perpetual danger of relapse. Progress is this resistance at all stages, not the surrender to their steady ascent."[23] Progress for Adorno, then, demands that we not conceptualize it once and for all in the name of the ideal of humanity in which it seeks to make itself true.

Reconsidering Nationalisms: Feminism and Anti-Militarist Ideals   6

We all remember the pictures in the newspaper of smiling Afghan women freed from the brutal imposition of the *burqua*. We were called to celebrate their freedom because part of the Bush administration's justification for the war in Afghanistan was the freeing of subjugated Afghan women. A number of feminist organizations donned *burqua* pins to show solidarity with their "liberated" sisters. After all, the Taliban regime had brutally oppressed women, shocking the world with public assassinations and floggings of women for the smallest infractions. Who would not celebrate their downfall? What feminist would not consider the demise of the Taliban regime a victory for feminism? In an article in *Ms.* magazine, this pervasive feminist sentiment was expressed by calling the interim government in Afghanistan a "Coalition of Hope."[1] But on April 20, 2002, the Revolutionary Association of the Women of Afghanistan (RAWA) assailed this position of the Feminist Majority of the United States. They wrote a response to the *Ms.* magazine article, accusing the authors of ignoring the horrible atrocities committed by the Northern Alliance and for erasing RAWA's historical role: twenty five years of relentless struggle against the Khalq and Parcham regimes, local leftist parties dominated by the USSR, the Soviet invaders, the jehadi rulers now called the Northern Alliance, the Taliban, and once again those same jehadi rulers of the Northern Alliance who destroyed the major cities between 1992 and 1998.

In its response to the *Ms.* magazine article, the RAWA posed a set of penetrating questions to U.S. feminists:

> Are they merely mirroring the United States government and Western press who find it easier to present the Taliban as evil and the forces that

the United States supported against them as good? Or have they joined with our government in a concerted effort to ignore these crimes and once again forfeit the lives and rights of women for our current national self-interest. Perhaps the Feminist Majority, in their push for United States political and economic power, are being careful not to anger the political powers in the United States who still deny and make apologies for the human rights abuses done by the likes of Massoud, Rabinni, Dostum, Hekmatyar, and others who were trained, armed, and supported by the United States during the Cold War years in Afghanistan, and then left in a power vacuum to destroy their people and their country.[2]

RAWA does not here cite the innovative philosophical work of Giorgio Agamben, someone who has tried to show the contemporary political relevance of the ancient Roman category of *homo sacer* by claiming that "[w]hen their rights are no longer the rights of the citizen, that is when human beings are truly *sacred*, in the sense that this term used to have in Roman law of the archaic period: doomed to death."[3] But for the members of RAWA, their erasure is inseparable from the U.S.-led war in Afghanistan in which the innumerable deaths of Afghan citizens did not count, could not be counted, either in a moral or a mathematical sense. For we still do not know how many people have died as a result of our militaristic effrontery, people who were killed with impunity as *homines sacri*, people who looked up at our planes not knowing whether packages of aid or bombs were about to fall on their heads. For RAWA, the sacrilege of U.S. feminism remains its failure to acknowledge and assume responsibility for the suffering of the Afghan people and to see the truth beyond the veneer of liberation.

RAWA has fought long and hard against the inhumane treatment of women. And today it remains the leading organization in the struggle for democracy in Afghanistan because it is one of the very few organizations left politically unmarred by Islamic fundamentalism. By tirelessly fighting against the Soviet invaders, RAWA earned a strong reputation in Afghanistan and the refugee camps in Pakistan as exemplary patriots. Most of the members of RAWA—at least those who have not been executed or forcibly exiled—remain in Afghanistan or in refugee camps in Pakistan, seeking support for their own program of secular democracy, women's rights, and the re-establishment of a working infrastructure, which is utterly necessary for anything resembling a democratic society to thrive. Although RAWA is an organization for women, there are almost as many active male supporters as there are female members. One reason for this support is the breadth and depth of RAWA's political activities. Still, no one can become a supporter of RAWA without learning the central lesson of women's equality. As Esmat, a male supporter explained, "I've always found RAWA an organization that has disclosed the criminals and their real natures and faces in a situation where no one else did that, especially under the Taliban and jehadis. I am also proud of being a supporter of such an organization or even to know that such an organization exists. . . . RAWA through its website and the Internet worked a lot to disclose these faces and I think that through disclosing not only fundamentalism but also Khalq and Parcham and the Soviets, RAWA paved a way for women of Afghanistan to brighten the future for themselves."[4]

Throughout its history as a feminist organization, RAWA has been determined to "chant the slogans that are stuck in people's throats; to speak the words which others don't dare speak."[5] Its members and supporters have expected no less from their sisters in the United States, whose living, working, and political conditions are rather idyllic compared to those RAWA has been forced to endure since its inception as an underground organization. Anne E. Brodsky notes that "[a]s of fall 2002 in Afghanistan, under the transitional government, women are again in prison for the crimes of trying to marry the man of their choice, for seeking a divorce from an abusive spouse, and for failing to listen to the male authority figure in their home. Sharia law, imposing unequal penalties and burdens of proof on women and men, is still being used by the courts, and President Karzai has reinstated *Amr bil-Maroof wa Nahi An il-Munkir*, the vice and virtue police, who terrorized the people under the Taliban, to enforce Islamic codes of conduct on the streets."[6]

Although RAWA condemned the Bush administration for the bombing of Afghanistan and for its alliance with the vicious jehedis, its members and supporters nonetheless claim that people "should not be confused with their government. Many governments, without caring a bit about the values of democracy and human rights, helped create the fundamentalists by arming them and then leaving them to destroy the people. Then when the fundamentalists were out of their control, these governments waged a war against them, in which more innocent lives were sacrificed than by the terrorism of Osama and Taliban, and ultimately they gave the power back to the same old butchers. But in these countries are also the people who speak out against these policies and for whom the pains of our people are felt in solidarity; where even those feeling the agony of September 11 deep in their hearts went to Afghanistan to express their sympathy to the victims of American bombardment . . . our story can act as a beacon for many others who reflect our resistance and uncompromising stance against the bloody enemies of peace, security, and women's and human rights throughout the world."[7]

But RAWA's analysis of what happened in Afghanistan during and after the bombing forces us to question whether the humanitarian intervention discourse of the U.S. Government was not a particularly cynical effort to enlist U.S. feminists in an attempt to circumscribe the definition of what constitutes human rights violations—to turn the Feminist Majority into an ideological prop that delegitimatizes the political need for redressing human rights violations. The identification in the U.S. media of freedom with unveiling reinforced the simplistic view that the Muslim religion and freedom per se were radically at odds. RAWA's point to feminists in the United States is that we need to ask ourselves why we have been unable to heed their message and why some strands of feminism have actually been successfully co-opted by the Bush administration. Feminism is about listening to each other, supporting each other in our struggles for freedom and equality, believing that we must build our movements democratically—from the ground up—by paying careful attention to our sisters who are involved in the situations and conflicts we are called upon to support. Yet it seems that some U.S. feminists were decidedly anti-feminist—sexist, even—in their underestimation of RAWA as a feminist organization that was simultaneously an organization fighting for actual democratic emancipation and transformation in Afghanistan. Anne Brodsky ruefully describes a meeting of prominent U.S. feminists and a RAWA representative after 9/11: "Many people, regardless of their intentions or interest, clearly held a number of preconceived notions about how a 'third world' organization of Afghan women would operate. Some also made snap judgments based on what they perceived to be the youthful age of the traveling representative. All of this was in the air during that fall meeting between the mainstream U.S. feminists and the RAWA representative. Her hosts were concentrating on her as an individual and asking about her personal activities with RAWA. When Tahmeena said that her role as one of the traveling representatives grew out of her position on RAWA's foreign affairs committee there was a sudden lull in the conversation, as the other women in the room appeared to strain to integrate this piece of information into their mental picture of this young woman and her grassroots organization. Finally someone responded, 'A Foreign Affairs Committee, isn't that organized of you?!' There was an obvious tone of surprise and even condescension in her voice that an indigenous Afghan women's group would have a 'Foreign Affairs Committee'."[8]

The question of what role feminism should play in the global peace movement grows increasingly more urgent to address, especially in the wake of the wholesale devastation of Afghanistan and thousands of Iraqi civilians being doomed to death in Agamben's sense. We do not know exactly how many Iraqis are being killed and we probably never will, although the Bush administration, under pressure, has estimated the number of civilian deaths to be about 6000—a result of our cruise missile and aerial bombing attacks during the initial weeks of the war in Iraq. Some reporters in the European press have, on the contrary, suggested that there were 10,000 civilian casualties due to those initial bombings, while people in the devastated country of Iraq itself report to friends and relatives that it was much more than that. Those of us outside Iraq can only imagine the full extent of the causalities. Baghdad is in ruins. The "cradle of civilization" has been looted. Great treasures have been plundered and museums have been turned into tombs—a most tragic irony because it is usually museums, with their cultural artifacts, that offer us a record of what has been lost. All this destruction is claimed to be the result of the freedom we have given to the Iraqi people. We have righted the wrong of Saddam Hussein's brutal dictatorial regime. Or so we are told. As I write today, no transfer of sovereignty has taken place, and the resistance of the Iraqi people continues to escalate.

The overzealous hankering for global military and political dominance is by no means new in the history of U.S. imperialism—nor is the cynical justification that we pursue our aims in the name of humanitarian interests. In the recent case of the Taliban, the United States long ignored RAWA's call for international support for their efforts to bring to justice the Taliban leaders who had committed inhuman crimes against women. As RAWA is a grass-roots organization seeking real democracy in Afghanistan, for years there was no strategic value to the United States taking action against the Taliban on their behalf. Indeed, not only was there no U.S. support for RAWA, but the organization itself was seen as having a political agenda completely hostile to U.S. interests, considering RAWA's Marxist feminist commitments. Not only has RAWA been committed to the rights of women in Afghanistan, they have also had a dedicated commitment to international human rights. Indeed, RAWA has always drawn analogies between their situation as refugees and other women in the world who have to endure life in exile or in forced confinement in refugee camps.

In much of her Marxist feminist work over the years, Gayatri Spivak has shown that the long and brutal history of Western imperialism was able to survive, ideologically and otherwise, because the liberation of the poorest of the poor among women also helped promote a program of systematic economic domination. But recently, in an essay entitled "Righting Wrongs," she has shifted her theoretical focus, arguing that we must revisit the classical liberal distinction between natural and civil rights if we are to understand how it is that unjustified conceptions of natural right are used to encroach upon the civil rights recognized by nation-states in the global south and by de-legitimated social institutions and structures that grassroots activists are trying to revive and re-imagine. Her careful examination of human rights needs to be part of our "mistake meeting." "Mistake meeting" is a phrase coined by RAWA for those gatherings dedicated to reexamining their fundamental values and commitments as well as analyzing how their current work has promoted those values and commitments. Because I agree with RAWA that feminists in the United States quickly accepted a human rights justification for the war against Afghanistan, we particularly now need to hear Spivak's voice when it comes to some of the dangers of human rights rhetoric.

Spivak's point is that only once grassroots institutions and structures, like those built by RAWA in Afghanistan, receive new legitimacy can the nation-states in which they function overcome the human rights dependency that endlessly reproduces the figure of the "wronged victim"—a dependency that, according to Spivak, "can be particularly vicious in its neo-colonial consequences, if it is the state that is the agency of terror and . . . [Europe and the United States] that is the savior."[9] This self-permission for continuing to right wrongs is, for Spivak, premised on the idea that "wronged victims" will never be able to help themselves, and indeed will always need to be politically buttressed from the outside, due to their necessarily inferior political status, which renders them at once unwilling and unable to participate in what the likes of Bernard Lewis and Samuel Huntington would call the modern civilized culture of democracy. Spivak goes on to suggest that the notoriously shaky philosophical foundation of natural rights—the idea that our rights as "men" are anterior to our civil rights as citizens—often goes unnoticed in human rights discourse. The reason for this, she claims, is that a decidedly Darwinian assumption underwrites much of that discourse, namely that those who are naturally the most human must shoulder the burden of righting the wrongs of those less-than-human peoples who do not fit into our modern, as well as classical, liberal conception of the rights bearing individual protected under the law. Nevertheless, Spivak fully endorses what I would like to call, following Immanuel Kant, the ideal of humanity. But she does so by admonishing those of us who are citizens of the United States and of Europe to unlearn our cultural absolutism, which is in fact our own cultural relativism and which includes our hegemonic conception of modernity, our conception of ourselves as the natural saviors of the world, the ones who are the most truly human and who are thus in a position to name what counts, and especially what does not count, as human. Here, Spivak echoes RAWA's poignant call to U.S. feminists to examine why we were able to avert our eyes from the devastation of the American bombardment.

It is important to note that, like RAWA, Spivak is not against human rights. She thinks such rights are necessary and sufficient, in particular historical contexts, for achieving the ethical goal of righting wrongs. But it is perhaps even more important to emphasize that central to her recent thinking, no less than to her political activism in India and elsewhere, is the idea that human rights activists must be constantly cognizant of the fundamental inequality that allows them to right the wrongs perpetrated against so many others in this world, particularly women. With her conception of worlding, she forces those of us residing in "the first world" to accept that we inhabit an imaginary world that is only too real, a world in which doing the right thing is horribly bound up with Social Darwinist assumptions about the natural power to name the human, the inhuman, the animal, the beastly. Spivak's sincerest hope is that we can salvage human rights discourse by suturing it to "a future to come when the reasonable righting of wrongs will not inevitably be the manifest destiny of groups that remain poised to right them; when wrongs will not proliferate with unsurprising regularity."[10]

Anything less than this "suturing" would merely return us time and time again to justifications of human rights founded upon some avatar or another of Social Darwinism. In view of Spivak's critique of Darwinian liberalism, let us return briefly to Martha Nussbaum's attempt to name basic human capabilities[11]—a forthright attempt to solve the dilemma of how natural rights conceived precisely as human rights could manage to trump civil rights and indeed justify overriding the sovereignty of nation-states. Although Nussbaum wishes to leave space for cultural interpretation of the basic capabilities, she believes it is possible to describe in normative terms the proper contents and functions of these capabilities, and therefore what it means to be a full human being. Amartya Sen,[12] in both implicit and explicit critiques of Nussbaum, expresses his disagreement with this kind of hierarchical value system of natural human rights over and against civil rights by insisting that the means and end of development is freedom—freedom to protect not only civil rights, but what the Marxist Spivak would call the social production and circulation of capital and value. At his most radical, Sen argues that human beings need to be able to assert some control over the means of production as part of the protection of their basic capabilities. But that is as far as he goes: he backs down from Spivak's more daring project of raising questions about how we might suture a new ethics of responsibility to the figure of the other, to its imagined agency in a world that cannot count the other—in all its *sacred* forms and incarnations—among its sovereign agents. However, Sen does offer a potential solution to some of the ethical problems Spivak finds attendant upon human rights discourse. In *Development as Freedom*, he claims that "it is best to see human rights as a set of ethical claims, which must not be identified with legislated legal rights. But this normative interpretation need not obliterate the usefulness of the idea of human rights in the kind of context in which they are typically invoked. The freedoms that are associated with particular rights may be the appropriate focal point for debate. We have to judge the plausibility of human rights as a system of ethical reasoning and as the basis of political demands."[13]

I think there can be a feminist alliance between Sen's endorsement of the centrality of freedom in development and Spivak's own endorsement of humanist education as she connects it to her rethinking of human rights. Indeed, I want to assert that feminism must be thought of as inextricably linked to an uncoercive political process of suturing the habits and values of radical democracy onto cultural and ritual formations of the grassroots women's organizations. Such is the theory-driven feminist practice that Spivak herself has undertaken so painstakingly by helping to establish schools for aboriginal children in rural India, and by working with grass-roots women's and human rights groups that seek to weave together—not unlike RAWA—gender politics, the struggle to survive, and the actual formation of democratic organizations. But we cannot undertake this kind of work in our own countries and throughout the world without creating feminist ethics anew. We need to refashion human rights discourse so that at its core there is an ethical moment of reflexivity—our own vigilant self-reflection on the dangers of any individual, nation-state, transnational institution, or even NGO claiming that it is in a position to turn the ideal of humanity into something that can be given hierarchical and, hence, non-ideal shape. Most importantly, we cannot allow the ideal of humanity to be used as something that those who usurp the sovereignty of others, subsuming it into their own, will use to render some *homines sacri* whose lives will not count among those who are living as politically legitimate human beings. RAWA calls us to see this project as the heart of what might genuinely be called transnational feminism.

To understand the power of RAWA's feminist practice and their struggle for national liberation and democratic emancipation, I want to look more deeply into how women and symbolic articulations of the feminine lie at the heart of many efforts to consolidate nationalist projects, whether in the sense of imagining and creating a people or in organizing that people as a nation to develop a territorially bounded and legally established state. Let us first acknowledge that the struggle for national consolidation and the establishment of a state can be radically at variance with each other. A famous example of the founding of a state that fragmented national identity is Lebanon.[14] In Lebanon, citizens only belong to the state through their position in a religious community. The state institutionalized a national identity that was in religious fragments and these fragments used women and the protection of patrilineage to maintain the existence of proscribed identities. On the other hand, women also often identify with both the national community in Lebanon (which includes Syrians, Palestinians, and Lebanese) as well as a supranational community (which includes Arabs, Pan-Christians, and Pan-Muslims). Although proposals to change these identifications are now being circulated, the reality is that the religiously bound and patrilineally contained religious identities do not allow women to confer Lebanese citizenship on their children. The reason is that, given the religious institutional- ization of citizenship as a series of competing and, for many years, war- ring sects, such recognition of women's ability as citizens of Lebanon to bequeath national identity as a matter of political belonging would completely disrupt the masculine genealogy upon which the state had organized the nation.

This is an obvious example of women being used to perpetuate the purity of religious identities—for women are the reproducers of the chil- dren of those identities but with no power to have rights over their own children and indeed to allow themselves or their children to pass from one religious sect to another. But there are more subtle examples of how women are crucial to the constitution of the state and the construction of the ideal of the nation. Certain strands of Chicana feminism, for example, have brilliantly shown that the role of actual women as reproducers of the nation and as iconic representations of mythological figures ensconced at the helm of the nation-building project are bound up with what Jacques Lacan would have called the psychical fantasy of woman. There are the good women, the mothers of the nation who reproduce its citizens and mourn for their fallen children in times of war. To be sure, their mourning as good mothers of a particular state must have a proper object—namely, heroes and ordinary foot soldiers killed in the course of defending their country and, of course, idealized in their role as protective patriarchs for good women and children.

We all know Benedict Anderson's famous argument that nations are imagined communities.[15] However, in the case of the Chicana nation Aztlan, the organization of the nation is currently imagined without a polit- ical movement to claim territory,[16] although in its initial proclamation of the imagined home of the Chicanas there were some within the move- ment who sought to territorialize Aztlan by reclaiming the Southwest of the United States and thereby disrupting the articulated unity of the United States as an actually coherent territory. Some Chicana feminists have even argued not only that national desire territorializes itself through the putative naturalness of the people to which the land belongs, but also that it uses the imagined possession of women and their repro- ductive patrilineal line as the basis for a cultural group or identity being able to assert that "This land is ours." These feminists have sought to challenge the masculine and hegemonic roots of Aztlan by insisting that it remain, in Laura Elisa Pérez's words, "a utopic model of the homeland in that no-place that is everywhere embodied in discursive and other cul- tural practices."[17] This insistence, however, is inseparable from the work of Chicana artists, writers, and literary critics that, in different yet related ways, re-imagines the figures of Aztlan. These figures are borrowed from the long history of Mexico and its fight for independence, and include the famous figure of the good mother—the virgin of Guadalupe (*La Virgen de Guadalupe*), the imaginary mother who, in her purity, devotes herself to the nation. The Chicana artist Ester Hernandez has transformed this figure from weeping mother and warrior's sidekick into a defender of the Chicana woman as a warrior in her own right, struggling for her political rights as well as for those of the constantly re-imagined nation of Aztlan. "In this representation," writes Perez, "the central image of the Virgin (along with the metonymic chain of her attendant 'virtues' central to the reproduction of patriarchy and colonialism) is displaced by that of a Chicana warrior in karatea garb. The mark of the sacred, the enveloping aureola, is appropriated and transgressed in one gesture, for the new female image is marked as a new ideal through its familiar signs of venerability, while its received construction is pierced, as by a warrior's sidekick."[18]

On the other side of Lacan's psychical fantasy of woman, there is the indigenous woman, often imagined as the dark or beastly woman who disrupts the quest for national unity. The most infamous among such women is Malinche, purportedly Cortez's translator and mistress who sullied the "purity" of the people by creating *mestizas*. The term *mestiza* has been reappropriated by Chicana feminists in order to demonstrate how that name can be inverted as a symbol of resistance. This inversion, it is claimed, produces cultural and political multiplicity that allows *mestiza* consciousness to re-imagine Aztlan as irreducible to an exclusionary nationalism that rests its claim to legitimacy on an ostensibly pure people. As Norma Alarcón argues, "[t]he native woman has many names . . . [But] the point is not so much to recover a lost 'utopia' or the 'true' essence of our being, although, of course, there are those among us who long for the 'lost origins,' as well as those who feel a profound spiritual kinship with the 'lost'—a spirituality whose resistant political implications must not be underestimated, but refocused for feminist change . . . The most relevant point in the present is to understand how a pivotal indigenous portion of the *mestiza* past may represent a collective female experience as well as 'the mark of the Beast' within us—the maligned and abused indigenous woman."[19] *Mestiza* consciousness is therefore inseparable from how the feminine is deployed in projects of nation-building—for such projects inevitably entail the imagination. But it also is inseparable from the project of reclaiming the nation from the political imaginaries that resolutely separate women into the good, silent woman and the "whoring" woman (as in the myth of Malinche).

If feminine sexual difference is not to suffer abjection in exactly this figure of "the beast within us," then feminists within struggles for national liberation must protect the symbolic space in which the meaning of women can be re-imagined and re-defined without reserve. Chicana feminists have been exemplary in this effort to protect that space as crucial to salvaging nationalist aspirations from myths of ethnic purity. I continue to call this space the imaginary domain. Feminine sexual difference is undoubtedly in part an imaginary creation. However, the political and cultural discourses that give it meaning and the materialization of that meaning constrain the bodies and minds of actual women. The re-imagining of the feminine through actual images and icons, as well as changing the imagined ideal-izations of the good woman and her proper role in the nation, are crucial to how nations consolidate themselves and the different forms of national-ity they adopt in imagining how the state will be constituted and what it will embody. This kind of imaginative feminist political theory is indis-pensable to those currently challenging the Bush administration's attempt to bolster a nationalism that re-imagines "America" separate from the ideals of the U.S. Constitution. Women as idealized good women who mourn their proper objects—the fallen soldiers of the war against ter-rorism—have been deployed to support Bush's infinite war on terror and the continuing curtailment of our civil rights. It is because the good woman mourns her proper object that she reinforces the us/them divide that pits the good nation against the evil enemy. This makes mourning itself, and how it is connected to imaginary figures of women, important politically. Thus, public mourning for the other—the 'enemy'—can disrupt precisely that deployment of the psychical fantasy of woman that occurs in the name of horrific nationalist aggression.

In January 1988, only one month after the first Palestinian *intifada*, a small group of Israeli women, deeply disturbed by Israeli aggression against Palestinian resistance, decided to take action. Once a week, at the same hour and in the same location (a major traffic intersection), they donned black clothing and raised a black sign in the shape of a hand with white lettering that read, "Stop the Occupation." Week after week, they stood there in silence, cars zipping by them in every direction. The sight of women so boldly ignoring traffic regulations and making a dis-play of themselves in public streets caused traffic jams. As is often the case in grassroots women's movements, the message of this first vigil in Israel spread by word of mouth, women telling other women about what they had seen and its powerful effect on them. By the spring of 1988, there were over a dozen vigils organized in Israel that practiced, albeit in different ways, the form of bodily expression adopted by the first women who stood in black in the intersection. In Israel and Palestine, Women in Black continue to demand the complete evacuation of Israeli troops from Palestine and, at the very least, the acceptance of the cre-ation of a Palestinian state based on the pre-1967 war borders between Israel and Palestine.

Women in Black emerged in a nation engaged in militaristic aggression against a so-called enemy people, the Palestinians. It was the refusal of the traditional national boundaries—the distinction between enemy and patriotic loyalty—that fueled the Women in Black vigils from the beginning. News about these vigils quickly spread to other women residing in aggressor nations whose governments were engaging in nationalist and ethnic violence. Women in Black committed themselves to the belief that an alternative feminist politics was strong enough to militate against governments bent on war-mongering foreign policy. In Serbia, for example, Women in Black stood bravely in public plazas in Belgrade as the Serbian government disseminated racist propaganda about Serbian ethnic superiority, which fueled Serbia's nationalist campaign of ethnic cleansing. These Serbian Women in Black engaged in the very form of vigil practiced in Israel: they stood silently with signs and protested all forms of Serbian national aggression. Yet they also engaged in much more explicitly performative acts, including singing and dancing. During their performances, the women embraced the very names they had been called by their "good" nationalist men—traitors, sluts, lesbians, and whores; in so doing, they refused the abjection the names otherwise seemed to imply.

Today, Women in Black can be found throughout the world. In Germany, Women in Black demonstrate against neo-nazism, demand full citizenship for guest workers, and relentlessly insist that Germany remain fully disarmed. In India, Women in Black hold vigils that call for an end to the ill treatment of women by religious fundamentalists; they also unite with their sisters in Pakistan and thus bridge the many political, religious, and ethnic divides between India and Pakistan. So the question arises: How have Women in Black been able to unite women all over the world, including precisely those women whose respective nations are embroiled in aggressive military campaigns against each other? Quite simply, the power of Women in Black lies in their ability to assume the stereotypical positions of women and to re-imagine them in public and hence visible places. "The streets are ours": for years, this has remained the political platform of Serbian Women in Black, because the streets are where women, according to the conservative Serbian nationalists, are not supposed to "hang out," unless they are prostitutes. Good women stay at home, taking care of their families, not demonstrating their opposition to ethnic nationalism.

Yet Women in Black challenge the classical liberal distinction between public and private in an unusual and daring way: they take their politics into places where women traditionally conduct the day-to-day business of life—the supermarkets, the post-offices, and the schools. They show that these so-called women's places are potentially radical places of political protest and symbolic expression. In one of their most famous performances, Serbian Women in Black unrolled two long scrolls in a public shopping area in the center of Belgrade. One scroll read, "I confess"; the other, "I accuse." They encouraged people to stop and write on the scrolls their views concerning Serbian militarism and the brutal war against peoples of the former Yugoslavia. Unaccustomed to being treated as though their voices mattered, many women stopped shopping and took the opportunity to articulate in writing their deepest political and ethical convictions.

The very idea of Women in Black dressing in black is meant to convey the profound sense of resistance to a globalization that does not allow the demand for the ideal of perpetual peace to be heard. Indeed, as the very first vigils tried to make clear, Women in Black are imitating two seemingly polarized aspects of the globalized world: Manhattan black, the color of the happening, eminently fashionable woman, and the black that, throughout the Balkans and in many parts of the world, continues to represent women's duty to mourn. Representing these contradictory elements of femininity *as* contradictory, Women in Black demonstrate how women's place in the nation-state as stereotypically defined by nationalism and militarism can be undermined through the aesthetics of representation. As one woman from Belgrade Women in Black described it, "[S]tanding still mute with transparencies as a specific form of body art which together with a political message recalls . . . the fact that the woman's body is the direct use and impact of the feminine principle. For the first time, after the big democratic vote that was realized in Yugoslavia, Serbia and the first multi-party elections in 1990, the resistance of women became visible."[20]

The increased visibility of women, the putting into question of the traditional notion of political space by turning women's places into places of political expression and at the same time turning mourning rites into public displays of political protest against aggression, Women in Black have accomplished all this by mobilizing the stereotypes of femininity against their use in the perpetuation of nationalist aggression. Indeed, Women in Black have been brave enough to challenge any exclusionary notion of who should count as a woman for the purposes of their struggle against militarism. Straight men, gays, lesbians, and the transgendered are welcomed *as* women as long as they have the courage to engage in what Women in Black call the body-thought of their politics and ethics. It would be a mistake, then, to think that Women in Black only mourned, as that would simply reinforce the stereotype of the feminine mother who has lost her children in war. The embodied politics of women, which includes the endless struggle to find new ways for the feminine body to present itself in public, also involves joyous celebrations that completely undermine the place of the good woman as the reproducer of the nation. Serbian Women in Black often quote Cassandra as her myth is re-told by the German feminist novelist Christa Wolf.

Women in Black are disloyal to their nations of aggression and militarism. No longer will they stand behind their husbands, fathers, and brothers if these men choose to engage in horrifying militaristic aggression against other human beings. Most Women in Black take part in ritual mourning, it is true; but many of their international meetings have included celebrations of disloyalty to traditional patriarchal formulations of women's proper place that make lesbian marriages between women of warring nations the very heart of what is being celebrated. A Woman in Black from Belgrade recently described such a celebration: "The best example of these embodied activities and ideas are the international annual meetings of Women in Black: until now six encounters have been in Vojvodina, in different places, on a lake, in woods, under tents. . . . These three days were actually a rapture of joy and tears that through little sleep, much talk, music and wine brought to a catharsis. In 1996, in Novi Sad, a first public lesbian marriage, between an Albanian woman and an English woman, was celebrated with female/feminine rituals of dancing and singing."[21]

Joy and mourning, lesbian marriage, the celebration of a peaceful relationship to nature—all this is part of the body art and embodied politics of Women in Black. Because Women in Black all over the world practice a unique form of public mourning meant to disrupt the very idea and image of the good woman who mourns only for the lost soldiers of her own people, the infamy of their public mourning is inseparable from the way it performs the very disruption between woman and nation that is used in ethnic or patriotic feasts (as they are called by Women in Black) that devour actual people in a violent war machine. Both the politics and the ethics of Women in Black can be found in their mourning and their celebrations of women's powerful lives, both of which explode the traditional stereotypes of femininity. Such explosiveness is coupled with the full acceptance of the burden imposed by a belief in the idea that we cannot escape our humanity. That they heed the human call of political and ethical responsibility makes Women in Black one of the most important sources of wisdom, empowerment, and hope for all who desire a peaceful tomorrow and a better world.

The production of affect called forth in their mourning is inseparable from what Martha Nussbaum has recently called the judgment contained within the content of emotions.[22] Here, the judgment is that those who are enemy "others" are not cast outside the realm of the human, and that, therefore, their lives matter. Nussbaum distinguishes between emotion and affect because for her, affect—unlike emotion—does not involve "highly selective patterns of vision and interpretation."[23] The distinction

Nussbaum draws between affect and emotion undoubtedly turns on her suspicion of some of the deepest insights of psychoanalysis about drives and the unconscious. But if we fail to acknowledge the role of the unconscious, it will continue to dominate us and thereby prevent us from making sound judgments and evaluations about it. Yet despite this failure of acknowledgment by Nussbaum, her broad understanding of the cognitive basis of emotion entailing an imagined world is crucial for understanding how Women in Black can challenge a vision of the nation-state mobilized around ethnic superiority as a justification for wars of aggression. In Serbia, for example, Women in Black publicly mourned the victims of Bosnia, Kosovo, and Croatia and, in doing so, demanded that people challenge the nationalist imaginary that had reduced such victims to enemies fated to slaughter because of their supposed ethnic inferiority. Their public display of emotion was certainly part of a highly selective pattern of vision and interpretation that challenged the Serbian nation and its claim to be the true Yugoslavia. Nussbaum helps us understand not only that public displays of emotion have cognitive content in this broad sense, but also that there is political and ethical power at stake in Women in Black enacting all the conditions of a wake, including the shedding of tears over those who are considered unworthy of their weeping.

Although she understands the importance of the imagination in making the judgment that allows the emotion to be evoked in the first place, Nussbaum nevertheless fails to see that there is no easy analytic divide between the imaginary and the imagination, and that, moreover, we cannot be absolved of our responsibility to reflect upon how we might be captured by an imaginary that dwarfs our own ability to imagine and re-imagine. This failure becomes particularly important because Nussbaum insists that emotions simply attempt to fit the world. Women in Black publicly express emotions that do not fit their world, but that seek to transform the vision and interpretation of the need for war that certain nationalist imaginaries promote. They use public expressions of emotion to transform these imaginaries and rekindle the imaginations of the very people who have been captured by fantasies of their ethnic superiority or, in the case of the United States, their political exceptionalism. Thus, this distinction between imaginary and imagination is crucial for understanding the political and ethical power of Women in Black because they invite us to judge human beings reduced to the figure of the enemy as just that, human beings, not Agamben's *homines sacri*. When Israeli women bravely march into the West Bank and stand in silent vigil for fallen Palestinian men and women; when in New York another group of Israeli women hold up a sign tragically reminding us that, in the last five years, 62% of the Palestinians killed are under the age of 12, and weep for them and for their mothers, they are called traitors, whores, and lesbians because they refuse to treat those enemies as the worst beasts imaginable—because they mourn for them as human beings. The very image of the mother as the protector and reproducer of the nation is profoundly disrupted, and with it, the legitimacy of the aggressive acts that women are supposed to endure in the name of their proper place in the nation-state. Thus, the simple act of mourning is inseparable from recognizing the ideal of humanity. For every single human being who dies in war is a tragedy and one for which we must mourn.

Mourning is a political and ethical performance in Women in Black because it involves not only participating in wakes for actual victims, but also an act of what they simply call tenderness toward all others who can be mourned in their singularity, their infinite worth, their pricelessness. This performance acts out Jacques Derrida's recent claim that "dignity is of the order of what is called the *priceless*. What is absolutely precious, the other in his or her dignity, has no price . . . two human beings . . . have an equal moral, juridical, political *dignity* whatever their differences in all other respects."[24] The lesson here is that there is a deep and profound psychoanalytic connection between the imagined good woman and the imagined nation. This takes us back to my opening discussion of RAWA's attack on the U.S. Feminist Majority. The connection between woman and nation enabled the Feminist Majority to represent all "good" American women against the "bad" revolutionary outsiders RAWA, and, moreover, to legitimate the patently unnecessary bombing of Afghanistan in the name of feminist nationalism which was in fact a sacrilege of feminism. Radical feminists who are citizens of the United States must, then, dare to be politically infamous; they must be vigilant in insisting that psychical fantasies of women not be turned into a justification for preemptive U.S. military aggression against other nations—that preemptive strikes can never be justified in the name of saving women, especially when bombs fall on the heads of women U.S. military men are supposedly saving. As one Woman in Black from Serbia eloquently put it, "I do not see why we should not worry about 'our people' and 'their people' in the same way, because this exclusion of the other is at the roots of fascism, in the divisions between ours and theirs, me and the others and normal and abnormal."[25]

Women in Black are explicitly pacifist and have been criticized for an unrealistic pacifism. But since any three women who stand in black count as a vigil within Women in Black, there are many different positions: some explicitly and generally pacifist, others with more specifically focused strategies of resistance. The power of Women in Black is that they refuse traditional definitions of the good woman supporting her men in time of war. Not only do they challenge limited articulations of feminine sexual difference within the constraints of normative heterosexuality and its corresponding kinship systems, but also seek forms of solidarity with the so-called enemy in the name of trying to develop a more sweeping program of anti-militarism. In this sense, they have moved toward something like a universalizable principle for anti-militarist and anti-nuclear political organizing.

In Okinawa, Japan, a feminist organization called Okinawa Women Act Against Military Violence (OWAAMV) has explicitly developed a program for security very much in the spirit of Women in Black. Their program has four main principles:

> The environment in which we live must be able to sustain human and natural life;
> People's basic survival needs for food, clothing, shelter, health care, and education must be met;
> People's fundamental human dignity and respect for cultural identities must be honored; and
> People and the natural environment must be protected from avoidable harm.[26]

After the U.S. military established its base in Okinawa after World War II, Japanese women began organizing around the tragic rapes by U.S. soldiers that have been a constant occurrence ever since. Although the official U.S. occupation of Japan ended in 1952, Okinawa remained under direct control of the U.S. military until 1972. Even to this day, it is one of the largest U.S. military bases. Although the United States no longer directly controls Okinawa, its military presence dominates the entire island. The cost of this military base to women and children is not only continuous rapes and sexual assaults, but also environmental poisoning. This is why part of OWAAMV's new program for security involves environmental testing and clean-up. The United States and Japan have agreed to start transferring military facilities to civilian control. But many NGOs remain concerned about the responsibility the United States must accept for environmental clean-up before these facilities can be safely transferred.

Okinawan feminists have also worked to create the East Asia-U.S. network against militarism, which requires that U.S. women take responsibility for what the United States has done in Okinawa and to struggle with East Asian women for the new paradigm of security that OWAAMV believes can be a universalizable program. The move from traditional issues of women's concern—such as rape and sexual violence—to the question of building a transnational network and a new paradigm of security demonstrates that, because feminism challenges basic kinship arrangements that ground nationalist and militarist institutions, it opens up space for universalizability in the very course of its struggle. In other words, Okinawan feminism sees the connection between certain fantasies of women, particularly Asian women, and the way U.S. soldiers treat them. But their feminism cannot be reduced to getting a square deal with the men (in the sense of fair and equal opportunity) because all the people in Okinawa suffer from the presence of the U.S. military base. Thus, Okinawan feminism moves beyond formal equality in the very definition of how it sees its struggle against rape as integral to the de-militarization of Okinawa itself. Women can only be safe if Okinawa is freed from U.S. military presence: this is the insight that led to the OWAAMV-alternative anti-militarist program for security.

Of course, the word "security" is bandied about a great deal these days. It is politically important for feminists to answer the call for security, especially when we are told by the Bush administration that we must give up certain aspects of our basic constitutional rights in its name. The Okinawan feminist program for security, with its insistence on the connection of security to de-militarization and anti-nuclear struggle, is an alternative to the current rhetoric of security, especially at a time when the United States becomes increasingly responsible for the undermining of nuclear non-proliferation efforts. But both Women in Black and OWAAMV have shown us that feminism must be expressed in explicit calls for universalizable ideals like the Okinawan security program. At the same time, they also question current representations of humanity informed by fantasies about women's place in the nation and their relationship to militarism. By interrogating such representations of humanity and the normative heterosexual kinship structures connected to them, radical feminist theory and politics can challenge the construction of woman as a subordinate object in the name of a symbolic universality that opens up new spaces for rethinking how we can be human together, including how we might find something like lasting security and invest in the dream—the ideal—of perpetual peace.

Other Family Stories: The Ethics and Politics of Transnational Adoption 7

If you are an adopting parent, a birth parent, or an adopted person, you are part of the story of adoption; but you are also one of the people who shape the story. From the moment one decides to become an adopting parent, all the details of one's life are exposed to the legal systems of the states involved in the adoption process. The process of adoption, for an adopting parent, is about becoming passable and acceptable as a parent. For the mother who relinquishes her baby, it is very different: it is about divesting herself of her parental role. Adoption agencies and prospective parents frame children through the law and other political means. And while the frame establishes the scope of possible relationships and the stories that can accompany them, adoption stories and relationships can create new pathways of love that defy the exclusionary and hierarchical systems that seem to inform them in the first instance. To the degree that they ever become "ours," the stories and relationships of adoption are ones of disruption. They proceed from embattled engagements with the international and transnational institutions that pigeonhole citizens of the world into triangulated positions—birth parents, adopting parents, adopted children. These institutions create such a triangle through strict adherence to heterosexual and culturally specific norms of kinship—norms that, for many involved in the adoption process, are anything but normatively desirable.

My adopted daughter, Sarita Graciela Kellow Cornell, was born in Paraguay in 1992. I adopted her from Paraguay in April 1993. In 1997, my daughter became a naturalized U.S. citizen. At the naturalization proceedings, I was one among a group of several hundred adopting parents from the United States. After our naturalization papers had been verified, both the adopting parents and the adopted children were given flags of the United States and allowed to join a ceremony. The mood was celebratory. An official from the Immigration and Naturalization Services[1] congratulated us for our generosity of spirit, our good will, and our courage. After all, we had traveled to a "Third World country" to adopt our babies. As the official droned on, I kept imagining the struggle of Gladys Gomez to have her baby returned to her.

In 1996, Diane Jean Schemo wrote a *New York Times* article about how babies were being stolen in Paraguay, and described Gómez and her plight: "Gladys Gómez's shoes are torn, her fingernails ragged and her blouse threadbare. But the picture she keeps in her pocket, of the daughter who disappeared almost three years ago, is still crisp, wrapped in plastic like a personal shrine. Miss Gómez, 23, said she left her daughter, Cintia Carolina, then 14 months old, in the care of a cousin while she went to visit her godmother nearby on the night of Aug. 28, 1993. When Miss Gómez returned a few hours later, her only child had disappeared. Relatives told her that the cousin, who is being detained on charges of stealing the child, had sold Cintia for international adoption."[2] I imagine Gómez trying to get her daughter back. I imagine the horrible, earth-shattering panic and anxiety that her baby is gone and yet the hope that maybe she can be recovered. And then the tragic realization that she is gone. And then the radical absence and despair followed by the lost years she will never get back. But despite all odds and obstacles, Gómez remained determined. She did not give up and, at the time Schemo wrote her article, Gómez believed that she had discovered that a couple from the United States had adopted her daughter in 1994. But did she ever get her daughter back? I wonder. I try to reassure myself that I followed the letter and spirit of Paraguayan law. Sarita was not kidnapped. Or rather, Mabel Delgado Barrio was not kidnapped—that was the name Gabriella Delgado Barrio gave to the little girl I renamed Sarita.

I listen to the INS official talk about the adopted Paraguayan children having won in "the great lottery" of life because we had given them the ultimate prize, U.S. citizenship—a prize coveted throughout the world. The official presumes they would have had little chance for a meaningful life because of the poverty, cultural deprivation, and corrupt governments in their countries of origin. But the presumption goes one step further: "our" children were worse off than even "normal downtrodden, Third-World children" because they had been born to women who abandoned them and could not take care of them. The official is absolutely confident that this is a salvation story, and that these children have won. Clearly, Gómez did not think that the kidnapping of her daughter was an act of deliverance—either for herself or for her daughter.

After the speech, the parents read the citizenship oath because the vast majority of the children cannot read. I leave out the phrases that do not apply to my daughter. I had petitioned to have my daughter retain her Paraguayan citizenship. And the petition was granted. When she turns 21, Sarita will have to choose whether she wants to keep her Paraguayan citizenship. I want to get outside as quickly as possible to escape what I see as an orgy of disrespect for the diverse peoples' lives into which these children had initially been born. I go from feeling embarrassed, to guilty, to completely horrified by the thoughtlessness of the INS official who seems to have no idea of the political and ethical complexity of a transnational adoption. A transnational adoption implicates all the layers of global injustice that I try to fight against; but as an adopting mother, I am also a participant in this system. That is the inescapable paradox that Gayatri Spivak captures in her extraordinary phrase "enabling violation." Due to the horrifying economic inequalities that separate countries in the global North and the global South, many children are left in serious poverty. These inequalities are created and sustained by the very countries that allow some of us the resources to adopt in the first place. Thus, what can be enabling for certain children—parents who adopt them and, in many cases, enable them to stay alive—is inseparable from the violation perpetuated through systematic inequalities. Throughout her work, Spivak speaks of the post-colonial condition as itself an enabling violation. Being part of the scene of adoption forces us to acknowledge the great extent to which the post-colonial predicament is about the continuing legitimation of inequalities between northern and southern countries.

By 1997, I had realized that there was no avoiding the enabling violation inherent in a transnational adoption. Both my relationship to Sarita and the frame of that relationship had to be confronted. My critique of the official story does not prevent me from being part of the official story of Sarita's citizenship and U.S. global political hegemony. At the time of Sarita's adoption, I was scared of the adoption process, with all its state trappings. I saw this and yet did not see it. I had myopic vision: I could see only the next step in what seemed an endless process. Much of what I knew about the egregious inequalities that define so many of the relations between nations of the world blurred in the frightening whirl of the adoption process.

When I first arrived in Paraguay in April 1993 to adopt my daughter, I was troubled by the fact that I was on the wrong side of the adoption issue. I was staying at the Grande Hotel del Paraguay. It was a hot night. The street outside the hotel was full of demonstrators, who held up placards that exclaimed: "Yankees Go Home!"; "Child Kidnappers!"; "Paraguayan children for Paraguay!." U.S. citizens were told not to leave the hotel or they would be in danger. There was to be an election on May 9th. All the parties had one thing in common: they promised to outlaw all adoptions to the United States. I tried my best to hear the message of the demonstrators. It took two years for the new government to suspend adoptions to the United States. By 1995, Paraguay, a nation of only 4 million people, had become the largest supplier of adopted children to the United States. The suspension honored all adoptions that were in process. Paraguay was not alone in implementing anti-adoption legislation. The Hague Convention on the Protection of Children and Cooperation in Respect of Intercountry Adoption (THC) had been passed in 1995. The THC was recommended by The Hague convention on international law, which facilitates and oversees treaties. The goals of the THC are to "set minimum standards for intercountry adoption that will allow recognition among the party countries, protect the interests of children, both birth parents and adoptive parents and prevent illegal trafficking."[3] The United States has yet to ratify the THC. Examination of official U.S. Government statistics confirm that, between 1996 and 1997, Chile, Costa Rica, the Dominican Republic, Ecuador, Honduras, El Salvador, and Peru significantly diminished or banned altogether adoptions, regardless of whether those countries had ratified the THC. By the time of my daughter's naturalized citizenship ceremony in 1997, the existence of the THC already had a worldwide impact on the politics of transnational adoption.

Although it may be true to some degree that "wrong life cannot be lived rightly" (as Theodor W. Adorno wrote), most of us try to live life rightly, making judgments of right and wrong because we have no choice but to make them. I was thrown into the political and ethical fray of transnational adoption when I participated in Sarita's citizenship ceremony. I had to make a decision about how to proceed politically and ethically. I did not have the option of suspending judgment. I was an adopting mother but also a life-long leftist. These warring identities were the product of the enabling violation of the adoption process. I continue to tell Sarita the following: "You can live a good life in Paraguay if you want. You might well choose to do so. You have that option." The official story, of course, tells her precisely the opposite: only an adopting mother from the United States can give her a future; only assimilation into the receiving country will give her a rebirth and allow her to live happily ever after as a U.S. citizen.

The simple, linear narrative of assimilation may indeed be a soothing story to some adopting parents. Nevertheless, I suspect that many of the adopting parents I met at the citizenship ceremony felt as uneasy as I did at being cast as supporters of U.S. hegemony. They probably felt no less uneasy about the moralistic fervor fueling the notion that "children are being saved." After all, as soon as a child is brought from one country to another, the child's own life story inevitably changes. Indeed, in our thoroughly racialized society, a transnational adoption necessarily becomes a transracial and transethnic adoption. The new country deploys different markers of race and ethnicity that make the child conspicuously different from his or her adopting family. Until about 15 years ago, parents and children were matched so that the adopting family and its new child looked "as if" it were a natural family. No one was supposed to see the difference. And the adopting families could only be a "normal" heterosexual couple with women accepting their "proper" domestic role. In other words, women who wanted to adopt could not work. Single mothers were out of the question as prospective adopting parents. Gay, lesbian, and transgendered parents were also completely excluded because, by definition, they did not remotely resemble the "normal" heterosexual couple. Transnational adoption of children of color creates families that cannot pass "as if" they were natural families. In this way, both the U.S. naturalized citizenship ceremony and the "American" assimilation narrative belie the full impact and complexity of the prefix "trans." As Aihwa Ong notes, "Trans denotes both moving through space and across lines, as well as changing the nature of something. Besides suggesting new relations between nation–states and capital, transnationality also alludes to transversal, the transactional, the translational, and the transgressive aspects of contemporary behavior and imagination that are incited enabled and regulated by the changing logics of states and capitalism."[4]

Transnational adoption thus shows how idealized the traditional adoption narrative is. This is important because that narrative is hardly innocuous. In fact, it has caused great suffering and what Betty Lifton calls cumulative trauma in adopted children, even in those adoptions that do not cross racial, ethnic, and national boundaries. Herself an adoptee, Lifton was one of the first writers to define adoption as a trauma for the adopted child and as a scene of haunting for all the people involved in the adoption. Lifton searched for her own birth mother and ultimately found her, even though her adoption records were sealed. Lifton has devoted much of her life to testifying to the inhumanity of "sealed records," particularly the way they erect a seemingly insurmountable barrier to the child's past. Initially, the public justification for sealed records was to guarantee that children could avoid being labeled illegitimate. As Lifton explains, "The original purpose . . . was to protect the newborns from the stigma of being born out of wedlock . . . Social workers urged the courts to seal away the baby's birth certificate, which was stamped illegitimate, and to issue an "amended" one that substituted the names of the adoptive parents for those of the birth parents. As the policy of sealing records spread rapidly from state to state after World War II, however, it lost sight of its original purpose and became a means of protecting the adoptive family from interference by the birth family. Secrecy effectively pitted adoptive mothers against birth mothers and kept adopted children separated from their birth families."[5]

In the justification that the birth mother's privacy is being protected, we still hear the echoes of the purported shamefulness of the act that brought the illegitimate baby into the world. In Lifton's own case, her birth mother did not want to meet with her publicly because she did not want her son or even her neighbors to know of her shameful past. The secrecy is a symptom of the culture of legal normalization in which certain children and parents are deemed illegitimate, while others are not. Although the problem remains with us today, many birth mothers, adopted children, and adopting parents organizations have fought against sealed records and, increasingly, states accept open adoptions or at least give information to adopted children about their birth parents. But these changes have only occurred within the past 25 years. Lifton's own analysis of the dilemma of adoption sometimes wistfully yearns for a story other than the one she describes as a ghostland. Lifton thus ends her memoir with "What if all these things came to pass: unsealed and updated records, agencies treating adoptees as clients instead of enemies, adopted children knowing that when they are grown they will have the chance to search out their origins freely? I tried to imagine what those future adoptees growing up in such utopian circumstances would be like. Already I envied them. Or would they have problems too?"[6]

But her engagement with the story of adoption as she both lived it and as it was passed down to her contains a highly imaginary world of idealized heterosexuality and lineage. As Lifton muses, "A friend of mine recalls that when his seven-year-old (biological) daughter was a little younger, she would approach him four or five times a year with 'tell me the story.' And then he would tell her once again about how he met her mother through a friend, and how they started dating, and how they got married, and how they loved each other, and how she began growing in her Mommy's tummy. It made his daughter very happy and secure to hear the story that began not with her but with her parents who created her. Sometimes her grandparents and other relatives showed up in the details of the story of before she was born. The child knew without having to be told that her narrative was connected to the narrative of her parents, grandparents, and great-grandparents down through the generations, and so she was connected. Her narrative revealed her identity. It told her who she was. If there had been essential people missing from her narrative—her Mommy, Daddy, grandparents, and other members of her clan—it would have been difficult for her to feel as connected as she did. For most children, like my friend's daughter, their narrative is as much a part of them as their shadow; it develops with them over the years and cannot be torn away. Unless, of course, they are adopted."[7] For Lifton, her adoption breaks the chain of narration because "the Mommy and Daddy and baby makes three" is the narration of "normal," non-adopted children. It is the bio-logical bloodline that holds the story together. What is broken for her, though, is precisely this family lineage. And yet this brokenness, this shat-tering, would occur regardless of whether adoptions were open. Lifton recognizes that other traumatic situations can break up the family line: divorce, war, famine, and so on. But her point is that the break—no matter what its cause—is in itself traumatic.

Indeed, for Lifton, adoption itself is a trauma because it breaks up the bloodline, which she idealizes as the origin of a coherent narrative of family and roots. This idealization leads her to view adoption as second best—a compensation for infertility—and adopted children as perpetu-ally suffering. Only in view of Lifton's claim that infertility is the main reason that parents adopt can we understand her sketch of the shadowy and ghostly scene of adoption. Specters and shadows hover around the loss of the normal heterosexual family. "Who are the ghosts? The adopted child is always accompanied by the ghost of the child he might have been had he stayed with his birth mother and by the ghost of the fan-tasy child his adoptive parents might have had. He is also accompanied by the ghost of the birth mother, from whom he never completely dis-connected, and the ghost of the birth father, hidden behind her. The adoptive mother and father are accompanied by the ghost of the perfect biological child they might have had, who walks beside the adopted child who is taking its place. The birth mother (and father to a lesser extent) is accompanied by a retinue of ghosts. The ghost of the baby she gave up. The ghost of her lost lover, whom she connects with the baby. The ghost of the mother she might have been. And the ghosts of the baby's adoptive parents."[8]

In the case of the adopted child, the "perfect" child her parents might have had accompanies her as a mirror of her own failure—her failure to be the perfect child for her parents. The adopted child comes to mimic the child who never actually existed, except perhaps as part of the uncon-scious fantasy in the psychic life of the adopting parents. On Lifton's account, this becomes futile mimicry because it involves buttressing the fantasy projected onto the adoptive parents at the expense of the adopted child's own separate existence. This is Lifton's "good adoptee," whom she identifies as herself prior to her search for her birth parents. Yet from within her own perspective of despair and despondency, Lifton imagines the adopted baby knowing that it can never be the real object of its par-ents' affection—knowing that it is a fraud: "Ideally the wicked changeling would be gone when the mother awoke, and in her place would be the good sweet, obedient child, all curly haired and dimpled like Shirley

Temple. Of course, the real child was never returned, for adopted children are permanent changelings who are doomed to impersonate the manners and fidelity of the natural child who might have been. As if she understood this the changeling fled into herself and, since fairies are shape shifters, this one assumed the guise of a docile daughter eager to please."[9]

This is an imagined picture of the adopted child's artificial self, divided not only from the fantasy child of her adopting parents' psychic life, but also from her own fantasy self of who she might have been had she stayed with her birth mother. If adopting parents deny their adopted child the right to discuss the actual history of her birth mother, the child identifies with the gap at the very heart of herself that prevents her from becoming a whole person. In this way, Lifton identifies the quest for the identity of the birth mother and the quest for a unified identity as one and the same quest. Once this quest is foreclosed to the child, the child becomes melancholic, holding onto her entire identity in the form of a lost object that never was allowed to exist. Although Lifton does not refer to Freud, traumatized adopted children are best understood as melancholic in Freud's sense. Let me be very clear that I do not agree with Lifton that adoption is in and of itself a trauma. Of course, it can become a trauma under the condition of sealed records. The ego fragility that Lifton often describes as characteristic of adopted children keeps the lost object intact precisely at the expense of the ego's own organization and growth. In his classic study of mourning and melancholia, Freud defines the distinguishing features of melancholia as "a profoundly painful dejection [and] abrogation of interest in the outside world, loss of the capacity to love, inhibition of all activity, and a lowering of the self-regarding feelings to a degree that finds utterance in self-reproaches and self-revilings, and culminates in a delusional expectation of punishment."[10]

Bringing this Freudian psychoanalytic insight to bear on Lifton, I would suggest that, for Lifton, the adopted child's loss of its birth mother becomes the loss of its own ego due to the ambivalence that underlies the child's relationship to its adoptive parents. Because Lifton does not speak of melancholia directly, she cannot confront her own view of her adopting parents as desiring a labyrinth of secrets from which she cannot escape. This is why, over and over again, Lifton claims that she is "indentured" to her adoptive mother. "[I]t is one thing to have a story," she writes, "and another thing to tell it. I could not put it on paper. The adopted child in me felt a traitor. The child reminded me that her adoptive parents had taken her when she was helpless and raised her with the innocent hope that she would never look back. The unspoken debt was to be paid with acquiescence and silence: It is a form of emotional indenture even though it is made in the name of love. Adoptive parents demand that their stories end happily ever after, although they must know that families with blood ties cannot be promised such a simple-minded plot, that even blood children must one day go off on their own lonely journeys of self-discovery."[11] Through melancholia, the adopted child at once colludes with and resists the secret. Indeed, it is this unique combination of collusion and resistance that distinguishes melancholia from mourning.

Freud notes that while many of the attributes of melancholia are shared by mourning, the loss of self-esteem is purely melancholic in origin. "Now the melancholic displays something else," he argues, "which is lacking in grief—an extraordinary fall in his self esteem, an impoverishment of his ego on a grand scale. In grief the world becomes poor and empty; in melancholia it is the ego itself."[12] The lack of self-esteem that Lifton describes as part of the good adoptee's emotional experience of indenture is inseparable from a young child's inability to express the ambivalence of early childhood. For Lifton, the adopting mother cannot handle the "truth." So the adopted child must conceal it from her. But of course, the truth of the child's origins is bound up with her unique history—her utter singularity. Paradoxically, under Lifton's tale, a melancholic adopted child's lack of self-esteem is an act of love directed at the vulnerable adoptive mother. Yet within the child's psychic life, this generates not only self-imposed erasure of the ego, but at the same time resistance to it. "If one listens patiently to the many and various self-accusations of the melancholic," Freud observes, "one cannot in the end avoid the impression that often the most violent of them are hardly at all applicable to the patient himself, but that with some insignificant modifications they do fit someone else, some person who the patient has loved or ought to love. . . . There is no need to be greatly surprised that among those transferred from him some genuine self-reproaches are mingled: they are allowed to obtrude themselves since they help to mask the others and make recognition of the state of affairs impossible; indeed they derive from the 'for' and 'against' contained in the conflict that has led to the loss of the loved object. The behavior of the patients too becomes much more comprehensible. Their complaints are really 'plaints' in the legal sense of the word; it is because everything derogatory they say of themselves at bottom relates to someone else that they are not ashamed and do not hide their heads. Moreover, they are far from evincing towards those around them the attitude of humility and submission that would alone befit such worthless persons; on the contrary, they give a great deal of trouble, perpetually taking offence and behaving as if they had been treated with injustice. All this is possible only because the reactions expressed in their behavior still proceed from an attitude of revolt, a mental constellation which by a certain process has become transformed into melancholic contrition."[13]

Melancholic contrition, rather than docility or the artificial self, most accurately, describes Lifton's account of the complex relationship of adopted children to their adoptive parents—a relationship that harbors within it both blame and revolt that cannot be expressed other than as collusion. The adopted child feels literally torn between collusion and betrayal. But because this contrition follows from a deep ambivalence of love and hate, it need not culminate in suicide. It can lead to forms of mania, some of which produce extremely active and successful, if over-driven, people. Not surprisingly, then, many of the adopted children who sought Lifton's counseling were people who led productive lives. But the forms of behavior that elicit considerable attention are those that Lifton associates with the forbidden self—problems in school, substance abuse, and criminal activity. Implicit in these forms of behavior, along with Lifton's evil changeling, is the self-berating confession that "I am a bad person." The revolt turns against the ego from which it emerged, thereby confirming its worthlessness.

When Lifton was 7 years old, her mother told her that she had been adopted and that her parents were dead. Lifton was ill with scarlet fever and her mother stayed by her bedside. From what Lifton remembers of the story she was told, her father was shell-shocked and her birth mother died grieving for him. None of the story was true, Lifton later discovered. Even so, when she was first told this fable, it did not give her comfort. As she simply admits, "From that day I felt apart from other people."[14] Adding insult to injury, her adoptive mother demands that Lifton become part of the secret and that it be kept from her adoptive father. Describing her colluding self in the third person, Lifton writes, "She and her mother are conspirators now. They are collaborating on a labyrinth, a fearsome maze worthy of the great Daedalus himself. The mother shows the child how to place the secret, her bull demon, in the center. Over the years the child will faithfully guard this monster of whom she is both ashamed and afraid; and only in the stillness of the night will she imagine wandering down those tortuous passageways to throw some part of herself to it. Sometimes the monster lies waiting there in the center of the labyrinth, but at other times seems to be one with it. The child understands that she is the sacrifice on which the monster feeds."[15] The secret is not just about concealment. It is also about a child being "unclean." In the system of modern adoption, Lifton's mother "had no such way of cleansing her adopted child of that evil deed that hangs over most adoptions."[16] In her psychic struggle against her own ambivalence and rage, the "sacrifice" of Lifton's mother becomes indistinguishable from her birth mother's evil "deed." The adopting mother effectively kills off the birth parents. According to Lifton's adoptive mother, the birth mother dies of grief. Therefore, the implicit message to the child was that her baby was not enough to keep her alive. Her birth mother abandoned her. But Lifton's adoptive mother cannot save her. Hence, both mothers are equally "bad."

Supplementing Freud's understanding of mourning and melancholia, Melanie Klein argues that a depressive position emerges in which a child cannot realign its good and bad mothers through the reparative work of the imagination. "Ultimately, in making sacrifices for somebody we love," Klein argues, "and in identifying ourselves with the loved person, we play the part of a good parent, and behave towards this person as we felt at times the parents did to us—or as we wanted them to do. At the same time, we also play the part of the good child towards his parents, which we wished to do in the past and are now acting out in the present. Thus, by reversing a situation, namely in acting towards another person as a good parent, in fantasy we re-create and enjoy the wished-for love and goodness of our parents."[17] The mother being split into good and bad is at once normal and desirable since it enables the child to find a way out of depending on its fantasized, omnipotent mother. Following Klein, I would suggest that, in our struggle to claim our own person, we all need an internalized good mother or some other good object in her place in order to heal the wounds of a split and divided ego. The state of mourning depends on an already-internalized field of objects in which the lost object can find its place. Thus, mourning is a repetitive struggle of both the loss of the fantasized omnipotent mother (the figure Jacques Lacan will later name the phallic mother) and the recovery of the mother as the child comes to link the image of the good mother with the actual mother that cares for her. Mourning repeats the struggle of the alignment of the lost object with the internalized field of good objects.

"While it is true that the characteristic feature of normal mourning is the individual's setting up the lost loved object inside himself," Klein argues, "he is not doing so for the first time but, through the work of mourning, is re-instating that object as well as all his loved internal *objects* which he feels he has lost. He is therefore *recovering* what he had already attained in childhood."[18] When this struggle is thwarted or blocked, melancholia ensues or what Klein describes as depressive states in which there is an inability to internalize good objects and a psychic forfeiture of the "good" mother. However, in normal mourning, "the early depressive position, which had become revived through the loss of the loved object, becomes modified again, and is overcome by methods similar to those used by the ego in childhood. The individual is re-instating his actually lost loved object; but he is also at the same time reestablishing inside himself his first loved objects—ultimately the 'good' parents—whom, when the actual loss occurred, he felt in danger of losing as well. It is by reinstating inside himself the 'good' parents as well as the recently lost person, and by rebuilding his inner world, which was disintegrated and in danger, that he overcomes his grief, regains his security, and achieves true harmony and peace."[19]

The difference between mourning and the depressive position for Klein turns on the ongoing work of imaginative reparation that sustains the affirmative dimension of identification. The reparative work of the imagination in mourning when there is an actual death, however, should not be confused with an easy repose in which we simply dream away the death of the person we loved. It demands rather that, through identification, we come to see that person both differently and more complexly. In this way, we can hopefully both forgive them and take responsibility for our own aggressive fantasies of the other person that may have wounded and injured her. At once ethical and imaginative, this labor is bound up with the psychic method of mourning that Klein describes. It allows the individual to transform her shattered reality into a better reality and a more promising future in which what is good about the lost object can be preserved in a different and higher configuration. There is no simple "reality-testing," as Freud called it, where the mourner comes to accept the object as lost. On the contrary, there is a re-imagined relationship with the object, which is recollected as part of a reality that must continue without the actual presence of that object.

In Lifton's case, her collusion with her "bad" adoptive mother against her "bad" birth mother prevented her from being able to repair or re-imagine her relationship with either one. When Lifton finally reconnected with her birth mother, she wanted a relationship with Lifton, although not one that could make Lifton proud of her. The woman did not want her other family to know anything about Lifton. Excited that her daughter had found her, Lifton's birth mother sent her a sentimental Mother's Day card. But Lifton's disappointment that her mother was not the strong, proud woman she had dreamt her to be turns into anger and then abjection when her mother—Rae is her name in the story—sends her a generic greeting card that celebrates Mother's Day. Lifton offers a characteristically ambivalent response: "She should have known there were no Hallmark Cards for a relationship such as ours. Imagine seeing on the rack in the drugstore tucked in among Get Well, Valentine, Birthday, and anniversary greetings, a section entitled: To the child I gave away or to the Mother I never knew. My card to her would read:

The day that's known as
Mother's day
Is Adoption Day to me
A Day for wondering and regret
In which again I see

That laughing little babe
Of yours
Who grew into the orphan girl
Who would search you out, Dear, one day.[20]

Lifton does not send this card to her birth mother. Tragically for
Lifton, she could not embrace either one of her mothers. And in death,
neither could be mourned. Hence the dedication of *Journey of the Adopted
Self*: "To the memory of my adoptive mother Hilda and my birth mother
Rae who might have known and liked each other in another life in
another adoption system."

Lifton frequently identifies with Oedipus, who sought after his birth
mother as a means of discovering from whence his unique being came.
Recently, Adriana Cavarero has argued that the story of Oedipus continues to resonate for us because of the connection made between narration
and the need to know the beginning of a story, the narration of a unique
and embodied life always beginning with the mother. "The story of one
man's life," Cavarero writes, "always begins where that person's life
begins. We are not speaking of Man in his disembodied and universal
substance, but rather of a particular man, a unique being who bears the
name of Oedipus. . . . [H]e was born of a mother. The uniqueness of his
identity, his daimon, has its origin in the event of this birth. . . . [T]he
link between personal identity and birth, according to Oedipus, is mate-
rially founded as it is indubitable. His daimon is rooted in his being born
of a mother, this and not another; a mother who, by giving birth to him,
has generated the 'seasons' of his entire existence, this existence and not
another. By being ignorant of the factual truth of his birth, he has been
able to believe himself to become another; but he was never able to
become another."[21] Here we are returned to Lifton's central anguish that
the system of sealed records keeps the adopted child from knowing who
she really is. It is important to note here that in her dedication, Lifton
perhaps unconsciously recognizes a different outcome for adopted children if they are allowed the chance to struggle through their own history with both their birth and adopting parents. Let me stress again that
it is the system of sealed records and normalized heterosexuality that sets
up a scene of melancholia rather than one of mourning. What is crucial
is that the child be given the material from out of which she can tell her
own story that allows her to confront and engage her own idealizations
and identifications with both birth and adopting parents.

Unlike Lifton, Cavarero understands that it is a loss of narration—not
the loss of an actual object—that creates the plight of someone who is
cut off from her own history. Cavarero complicates Lifton's own narrative
because Caverero's understanding of the narratable self can actually help

us understand that robbing a child of her story wrongs that child. Cavarero is careful to remind us that, with our birth, with the fact that we are born from the womb of one particular woman, our mother inaugurates our full exposure to the world as the unique beings we are. Carvero distinguishes the question of "who am I?" from the more abstract question of "what is a human being?" For Cavarero, as for many other feminists, this abstract question conflates the universality of humanity with the sexual and gender particularity of human beings, thereby identifying the masculine with the human and disavowing the feminine within sexual difference. Without being able to answer the initial question of "who am I?"—that is, the question of "from whom was I born?"—Lifton felt that she could not know, let alone tell, her story. The story of the "good parents" that the adopting mother told her, which was an attempt to give her a "legitimate history," ironically concealed her daimon from her. In the ancient Greek religions and mythology, the daimon is the identity that actually hovers behind us: others see it but we ourselves do not. It is the sign of our uniqueness. Cavarero beautifully defines uniqueness as follows: "[D]ifference is absolute because each human being is different from all those who have lived, who live and who will live. Not because she is free from any other; on the contrary, the relation with the other is necessary for her very self-designation as unique. We come to suspect therefore that the bad reputation from which the term uniqueness suffers, both in the moderns and the post-moderns, depends upon the erroneous way in which it is mistaken for an idea of romantic origin. On the contrary, in the uniqueness of the who there is no homage to the self-centered and titanic subject of romanticism. The who does not project or pity herself, and neither does she envelop herself within her interiority. The who is simply exposed; or, better, finds herself always ready exposed to another, and consists in this reciprocal exposition."[22]

At birth, the uniqueness emerges as the new baby is already a who that can be no one else even though the story of her life has barely begun. One need not sentimentalize the role of mothers or the difficult labor of giving birth to accept the fact that we are all initially tied to a woman and born through her labor, and that our existence as a self with a story includes this co-existence with her and thus her story. Nevertheless, this means that from the very beginning of our lives, our stories and subjectivities are already positioned by another. We can now understand the hopelessly sentimental story told to the 7-year-old about how Mommy and Daddy fell in love and "did it" under just the right circumstances. At a deeper level, we can understand why Lifton romanticized the story told to the child of her friends, for it is purportedly this story that allows that other 7-year-old to participate as a spectator in her own birth and retrieve at least some semblance of the unity that was promised by her birth. Because Lifton was denied, on Cavarero's account, the desire for one's story, she grasped on to any story to pick up a supposedly continuous narrative thread. We are dependent on others to help us enact our own projects of remembrance, which is why adopted children need to have access to their history and adopting parents must accept responsibility for providing such access. "Autobiographical memory," she claims, "always recounts a story that is incomplete from the beginning. It is necessary to go back to the narration told by others, in order for the story to begin from where it really began: and it is this first chapter of the story that the narratable self stubbornly seeks with all of her desire."[23]

The temporality of a narratable self bears within it a circular turn to the past, to the others who can return this promise of unity to us. Recognizing as our own the stories that others tell about us requires that we acknowledge the "you" who recounts what we cannot remember. Cavarero traces the desire of the narratable self to the inevitable incompleteness of the autobiographical memory. According to Cavarero, we know that we all have stories, that who we are is, at best, presentable as a unique story by our living through the very incompleteness of our own story, our shadow, our daimon: "Indeed, the first and fundamental chapter of the life-story that our memory tells us is already incomplete. The unity of the self—which lies in the miracle of birth, like a promise of its naked uniqueness—is already irremediably lost in the very moment in which that same self begins to commemorate herself. This loss of unity gets turned into the lack that feeds desire. If everyone who is born, from the start—and with a promise of unity that the story inherits from that start—then no recounting of a life-story can in fact leave out this beginning with which the story itself began. The tale of her beginning, the story of her birth, nevertheless can only come to the existent in the form of a narration told by others. The beginning of the narratable self and the beginning of her story are always a tale told by others. Poor Oedipus knows it well, he who would not give up that story for anything in the world. Oedipus is therefore special only for his misfortune, because there is perhaps no one alive who does not understand what an inalienable right this narration is."[24]

The desire for unity coalesces into an ideal that provokes and sustains the desire to hear one's story so that one can know that there is indeed an answer, if always a tentative one, because any narration must be sensitive to the question "Who am I?" The story sought sustains the promise of unity and a sense of a meaningful life. But the desire arises from the inevitable exposure of ourselves to others throughout our lives. Because we are exposed, we are at once narratable and vulnerable to others' narration of us. As Cavarero suggests, "It nonetheless seems to us that, more than immutability, it is the unity of the self made tangible by the tale, which moves the desire of the narratable self to seek the narration of the life-story. In other words, the narrative familiarity of memory, which constitutes the self as a narratable identity, has, in the unity of this identity, the ideal of her desire. The unity is therefore the figure of an in-born and inexhaustible tension; it is the design promised, from birth, to a unique existent, in so far as she exposes herself to the world, leaving behind herself a story. The one who is unique is also one in the very act of self-exhibition. She is this way first of all in her birth, when she is already a who without yet being a what; when, in her very new beginning, she is unique unity, about whom multiplicity, or fragmentation or discontinuity, cannot yet be predicted."[25] The who appears in the world both through the mother and through her withdrawal. In this sense, the orphan's ontological condition is simply a more fragile exposure: "This exposure is, in the case of the orphan, simply more fragile. The mother, who embodies the *ex-* of existent, despite having been there at the origin of the child's existence, is now no longer there. Existence as exposure becomes, in this case, the perceptible truth of every existent, made more acute by the immediate loss of one's own origin."[26]

We want our desire for a narratable self recognized by all others, but particularly by those on whom we depend for narration and memory. In this way, a closed adoption system does more than just wound a child, as in Lifton's case, by foreclosing the narratable conditions of its life. It denies the adopted child her desire for a narratable self. If the adopting parents are to be faithful to the desire for narration and selfhood—for a self with a story—there is an escape from Lifton's labyrinth. If they deny the child this desire, she will inevitably try to follow the clues that lead her back to her own history without ever knowing what she is looking for. "What does one do?," she asks. "Does one spend the rest of one's life playing Sherlock Holmes, following clues, looking in old phonebooks, rummaging through old records and graveyard listings, knocking all the doors of old addresses—hoping that some action will magically spring the lock which holds the door to the labyrinth? One does—there is no choice."[27]

It is the loss of the narratable self that is the trauma that Lifton describes. Lifton finds her birth mother; ultimately she finds someone who knew the story of her father and can narrate a version of her father's relationship to her mother. She can finally patch together her story, but only incompletely. It is not enough. At the end of *Twice Born*, Lifton is still waiting "for the Great Unsealing Day,"[28] because she cannot find a story that she can claim as her own. This vulnerability is more than just an ontologically more fragile experience of how we all are exposed and narratable because of that exposure. "I think about Jean's words for the adopted," she writes, "a lot in the next few months. Orphan. I never thought of myself as an orphan before. I go to the dictionary: an orphan is a child who has lost both parents through death . . . or less commonly one parent/an orphan is a young animal who has been deserted or lost its mother/an orphan is a person or thing that is without protection, sponsorship/an orphan is bereft of parents. Nowhere in the dictionary does it say that an orphan is someone who has been adopted. We [who are] adopted are not bereft of parents. Do we not have those 'psychological parents' who raised us? But now that I think about it honestly, the orphan wind has been blowing relentlessly through me all my years, although I've tried to masquerade about like other more insulated mortals."[29]

The only insulation comes from the "you" that initiates your story. Obviously, many biological parents fail to be that "you" that Cavarero believes is the one who ultimately sustains our story by telling it to us, making up for the lacunae in our own autobiographical memory. But adopted children in a closed adoption system are supposed to disavow their very desire for a narratable self. Indeed, it is this narratable self that becomes taboo. Lifton's adopting mother reinforces this taboo, causing a rift between them that never heals. By demanding that her daughter not ask her about her father and their relationship, Lifton's birth mother imposes her own version of the same taboo. Neither one could give her what she desired so desperately—her own story narrated to her by her mothers. Taking to heart the theoretical insights of Klein and Cavarero, we can see that, within Lifton's own imagination, reparation through realignment of the actual mothers with the good mother could not take place. That Lifton's birth mother was in "hiding" kept her from offering and exposing herself. Lifton describes a phone call to her birth mother where she actually hangs up because she knows that her birth mother does not want her half-brother to know about her. Howie, her half-brother, answers the phone: "For a moment I was tempted to say 'Hello, Howie, this is your sister" to blow everything. Instead I put the receiver down, just like the heavy breather. It was all so tawdry. Again I was the dirty secret, the bastard, the polluter who would put a plague on my mother's house if I were discovered. The resentment I thought I didn't feel toward her now overwhelmed me. Did she think, like Jocasta, that once she had put her baby out on the mountain she was truly rid of it? That it wouldn't return to fulfill the prophecy of her sin: reveal her as a fallen woman? Did all natural parents really think that signing the release form is the equivalent of making the baby magically disappear: Now it's here, now it's gone? How dare she! How dare she what? How dare she not be my strong, beautiful, fantasy mother!"[30]

For Lifton, the fantasy mother of her imagination was the Rae who actually struggled to hold onto her after she was born. Lifton imagines this mother as strong and determined, willing to defy society. Indeed, even after Rae put Lifton in an orphanage, she continued to see her. It was only after considerable pressure from the orphanage and social services that Rae gave her up. As a result, Lifton was not adopted until she was two and a half years old. The circumstances of Lifton's early childhood clearly disrupted the psychic trajectory in which the mother as lost object is slowly replaced by the mother as a whole—the mother as her own individuated person. Although I agree with Cavarero that we are all exposed at birth to the loss of our mothers in that her body is no longer part of us, I also agree with Klein that giving meaning to that loss has everything to do with how we avoid becoming melancholic. For Klein, we must lose the mother's body and later her breast. But we can live through this loss by introjecting good objects that allow us to risk love and to take responsibility. As Esther Sanchez-Pardo succinctly defines the Kleinian position, "All subsequent losses that threaten the precarious stability of this psychic system can be mimetically negotiated so to speak if the individual were reinstating his or her inner objects anew but with the backdrop of the memory that he or she once succeeded in doing it. The opposite holds true for manic-depressive states. The violence of sadistic impulses and paranoid anxieties does not leave room for establishing good (whole) internal objects. The individual is overwhelmed by the sense that there is nothing good to hold onto, nothing good inside, and therefore nothing to recuperate. The feeling of emptiness and nothingness that the melancholic exhibits is due to a failure in introjection and to the infinite doubts and uncertainties that assail a subject who was unable to firmly establish his or her good internal objects."[31]

That Lifton experienced a break in the process of introjection and projection is clear from her story. In her work on adoption, Nancy Verrier, an adoptive mother, argues that the very act of early separation leaves traumatic traces because the child develops a relationship with the mother in the late stages of pregnancy. Scientific studies are pursuing this connection and what it means for adopted children. One does not need to idealize pregnancy or essentialize its meaning to accept that the separation of adopted children from the mother's body is different and more traumatic than the separation experienced by children who continue to have that first love object in their lives. "Adoption," Verrier claims, ". . . is in fact a traumatic experience for the adoptee. It begins with the separation from his biological mother and ends with living with strangers. Most of his life he may have denied or repressed his feelings about this experience, having had no sense that they would be acknowledged or validated. . . . Somewhere within him, however, he does have feelings about this traumatic experience . . . he is wounded as a result of having suffered a devastating loss and . . . his feelings about this are legitimate and need to be acknowledged, rather than ignored or challenged."[32] But the question arises: can traumatic wounds be healed or at least acknowledged within the psychoanalytic terms of mourning and reparation? Clearly, the trauma cannot be worked through if it is simply denied. Verrier encourages adopting parents to allow their children the space to symbolize the specificity of their loss, even if this involves primordial fantasies of the remembered other mother. That the fantasies focus on the other mother is not surprising because it is her body that is lost and recuperated in fantasies. The adopting mother is entrusted with these fantasies and with the attempts at symbolizing the loss of the other mother in exactly Cavarero's sense. The child tells the mother these fantasies in order for the adopting mother to protect them and ultimately return them to the child as part of its story.

The adopting mother is both the storytaker and the storyteller. Part of the task imposed by adoption (understood as entrustment of the child's story to the adopting parent) is that the child's story be recovered as part of her relationship to her past, to her birth mother, so that the child can imagine herself as witnessing her own birth as the beginning of her unique existence. What is crucial, then, is the adopting parents' commitment to and recognition of the child's desire for a narratable self as irreducibly part of the unique self he or she is. Lifton becomes bitter toward her adopting mother because she feels that she did not care about her desire for narration and selfhood and instead distorted the facts of her story. The distortion was that Lifton was legitimate, and that her parents were dead. Everybody is given a good stereotypical role: her father is the good soldier, the mother the mourning wife. As a sanitized fictitious tale, the story made Lifton feel imprisoned in the role of a docile little girl who was not given the psychic space to take responsibility for her own aggression and reattach herself to her first love objects—her two mothers as whole people, separate from her.

Adoption agencies have long advocated some version of this sanitized story. The "official story" of the U.S. embassy is a classic example of the story of transnational adoption being sanitized. Cleaned up stories always violate the uniqueness of the narratable self. Lifton's unwillingness to abandon "the orphan" should be understood as part of her psychic rebellion against the social system that prevented her from exploring her desire for a narratable self and against her mothers who had internalized its values. Bitterly, Lifton pays heed to the adoption taboos embraced by her mothers: "Let us now pay homage to taboos: They guard the rituals of the community-birth, initiation rites, marriage, childrearing, burial against interference. They guard adoptive parents from natural parents, natural parents from adoptive parents, adoptees from natural parents, natural parents from adoptees. They guard everybody from everybody. They enable us to live in armed citadels safe from each other. They protect us from our deepest impulses, from that to which we are most naturally drawn. The violated taboo is programmed to avenge itself, but should it fail benevolent society takes over the punishment of the hapless offender. In my case I didn't need society: I was doing a fine job myself."[33] To lift the taboo clearly demands the end of the closed system of adoption. Within that system, an orphan holding onto the abjected part of herself can be understood as resistance; and the melancholic position of adopted children as rebellion against an unjust system that denies them their desire for a narratable self. Sanchez-Pardo defines the Kleinian understanding of the relationship between melancholy and systems of social exclusion and taboos: "The character of receptivity or exclusion of the external environment is decisive for the future adaptation or maladjustment of the individual and determines standards of health and illness. Melancholia arises as an acute response to the dangers and lethal traps which external reality threatens our objects of love, admiration, and idealization. In a desperate attempt to safe-guard the object at risk, its incorporation and preservation inside the psyche seems to be the most effective maneuver, but it has a very high cost. Along with the loss, the effacement of the object, a retreat of the subject from reality is also present in acute melancholic states—manic depression and involutional melancholia. Melancholia is a measure of the intolerance and rejection that external reality imposes upon the individual."[34]

In their recent essay on racial melancholia, David Eng and Shinhee Han argue that stereotypes of model minorities breed melancholia because they are determined by the necessarily failed mimicry of whiteness. The ideal Asian American is as close as a minority can get to being white; but in the very act of mimicry, whiteness remains unattainable. The stereotype itself is an ideal envisioned as a means of containing particular minority populations. As Eng and Han explain, "While Asian Americans are now largely thought of as model minorities living out the American dream, this stereotyped dream of material success is partial. . . . The success of the minority model myth comes to mask our lack of political and cultural representation. It covers over our inability to gain full subjectivities—to be politicians, athletes, and activists for example—to be recognized as 'All American'. . . . This near-successful assimilation attempts to cover over the gap—the failure of well roundedness—as well as that unavoidable ambivalence resulting from the tacit comparison in which the Asian American student is seen as lacking. This material failure leads to psychic ambivalence that works to characterize the colonized subject's identification with dominant ideals of whiteness as a pathological identification. It is an ambivalence that opens upon the landscape of melancholia and depression for many of the Asian American students with whom we come into contact on a regular basis. Those Asian Americans who do not fit into the model minority stereotype (and this is probably a majority of Asian American students) are altogether erased from—not seen in—mainstream society."[35]

Eng and Han's insight into racial melancholia is directly relevant to Asian American adoptees, with the added dilemma of these children being "sold" to white parents on the basis of their model minority status and hence their ability to assimilate more easily into mainstream white society. The story of immigration can never be the same for a child as it is for an adult because children seldom choose to immigrate to other countries. If white parents simply assume and demand assimilation from adopted children, then psychic conflict over loss and abandonment is not given adequate space for articulation and reparation. Coupled with the imposition of stereotypes of race and ethnicity, this conflict can clearly result in racial melancholia as the only possible position of resistance to assimilation. But what can be the beginning of institutional change that affords transnationally adopted children the psychic and narrative space in which to grapple with their own unique and frequently tragic histories? Obviously, a child's country of origin, along with the social processes of encoding racial and ethnic difference in the United States, has everything to do with the answer to this question. Yet as "sending" countries slowly come to terms with their historical roles as such, interesting experiments involving their grown adoptees in the diaspora have begun to occur. These experiments and the reactions of adoptive and birth parents to them will become part of the story of transnational adoption.

In 1997, the South Korean government welcomed South Korean adoptees back to South Korea, guaranteeing them a special class of quasi-citizenship. The ceremonies were called marriages and received much political attention. Some of the adoptees were Amerasians produced by the occupation of the United States in the Korean War. The "mixed" appearance of these children within South Korean society had been a reminder of the shameful U.S. occupation. But "Amerasian" children comprise only a small percentage of adoptions. Korea continued to have an extremely high rate of adoption until very recently. But South Korea's struggle to become a "modern" nation led to the decrease in adoption. Currently, its foreign adoptions are down to 2000 per year. Yet between 1955 to 1997, more than 197,000 Korean children were adopted overseas.[36] The wedding ceremonies were one way for the government to show that Korea was no longer the kind of country that would send away its own children. Many Korean adoptees felt stifled by these awkward ceremonies. But the stifling is inseparable from the forgetting of the trauma—that these children were sent away and that this is part of their story. In terms of the narratable self, the forgetting of the uniqueness of their history frustrates the desire of the adult adoptee to retell her story, which undoubtedly includes coming to terms with "Koreaness." Elena Kim has conducted a study of Korean adoptees and tracked their response to the government's effort to change its image and the meaning of being a "sending" nation. She argues that "[f]or some adoptees who go to South Korea, the past weighs heavily, whether as something to actively explore through birth family searches or as something to defer. Many confront their individual histories and understandings of cultural identity and belonging in ways they may never have done before. This sense of belonging is, of course, connected to 'Korea' as a nation–state and ethnic cultural paradigm, but it is also produced out of disjuncture with 'Korea.' The social memory of transnational adoptees is necessarily fractured and diverse, deterritorialized. And as Korean adopteeness is increasingly articulated by a collective, global and deterritorialized community, collective histories, constructed through shared storytelling, constitute a disidentifactory practice out of which Korean adoptees cultural citizenship emerges."[37]

Kim emphasizes the complex process of identification and disidentification—belonging to, being rejected from, and then being welcomed back to Korea. As she observes, "Common feelings of disorientation and alienation from Korean culture are expressed by adoptees who go back to Korea and desires for authentic personhood frequently surface in adoptee activities of self-narration. These narratives suggest that the ideal of building bridges, of being flexible 'citizens' or postcolonial hybrid subjects may be more compelling in theory than it is in lived practice."[38] In 1996, Korean adoptees, many caught between conflicting idealizations, held their first conference called The Gathering. The South Korean government idealized them as part of its own attempt at becoming a modern state. Some adoptees, however, were ostracized because they were viewed as radically different from other Koreans. Yet despite mixed feelings that were expressed, there was also an acknowledged sense of belonging to a society in which everyone looked like them. On the other hand, they spoke of their experiences of racism in the United States and the complex relationship to whiteness and the stereotype of the ideal minority Eng and Han so eloquently describe. "A survey of the participants at The Gathering," Kim writes, "found that 40% of respondents said they identified as Caucasian in their adolescence and perceived Asians as 'the Other.' For adoptees who grew up isolated from others like them and who identified primarily as Americans, therefore, racial discrimination posed a particularly difficult form of double consciousness. Even the most empathetic parents were perceived as unable to fully relate to the experience of racism, thereby intensifying feelings of alienation and racial difference. Some described it as a pendulum swinging back and forth between 'Korean' and 'American' sides. Many agreed with one attendee's sense that Koreans reject the American side, Americans reject the Korean side, adding that Koreans reject the adoption side."[39]

Well-meaning white parents who actively tried to get their children to pursue their Korean heritage were also seen as aggravating the alienation by remaining caught up in the orientalization of the adoptees' cultural and ethnic differences. Those white parents who tried to amplify the Koreaness of their children during adolescence were seen as only further exacerbating the problem of assimilation at an age when it was already proving difficult for the adoptees to identify and pass as white. The adoptees saw their parents' enthusiasm for their difference as just another indication of how they did not truly belong and how their parents did not understand the difficulty of identifying with that difference in a thoroughly racialized society. Because whiteness is the color that erases itself, the parents saw themselves as without a color, as without an ethnicity other than American. Thus, in the very attempt to recognize their children's uniqueness, the parents thwarted their need to identify as Americans "like them."

But The Gathering can be viewed as political if we follow Cavarero's understanding of the political as the space of exposure in which we make sense of our life stories. In the case of Korean adoptees, that story could only be told among themselves, because they were differently Korean precisely because of their history in the United States with primarily white identified parents. The Korean adoptee movement, according to Kim, "has been both a community-building project and a political one, exhibiting concerns with both cultural struggle and social policy. Sites of collective articulation and the searches for self and identity through different aspects of adoptees' experience contribute to what Teshome Gabriel refers to as a multi-generational and transindividual biography . . . a symbolic autobiography where the collective subject is the focus. A critical scrutiny of the extended sense of autobiography (perhaps hetero-biography) is more than an expression of shared experience; it is a mark of solidarity with peoples' lives and struggles. The Gathering . . . help[s] to illuminate some of the translocal conjunctures that form the broader context for the emergence of Korean adoptee heterobiography, constituted by discursive and symbolic practices."[40]

The Korean adoptees who gathered together presented stories different from the official story of adoption, whether promoted by the U.S. embassy (as in my daughter's citizenship ceremony) or the South Korean government. Their unofficial story challenges conventional notions of national and ethnic belonging, as well traditional patterns of heterosexual kinship. Although she observes the complexity of the response of Korean adoptees to the highly ritualized marriages between South Korea and adoptees in the diaspora, Kim also notes the importance of the South Korean government's attempts to open up space for Korean adoptees to further explore their relationship to Korea. Indeed, Kim recognizes that post-national hybridity may be a privilege for those who already take for granted a "home" in a nation-state: "In discussing issues of national identity with adoptees from

Germany and from France, I asked rather naively if they couldn't imagine themselves as being both Korean and German, or French and Korean. The French adoptee asserted: 'You need to be situated in a nation. It's too idealistic to think that you can live in between.' . . . [H]ybridity or dual belonging . . . is often felt to be an uncomfortable in-between state that is an undesirable or even untenable location. Unable to be fully 'French' in France or even American in the United States, they are likewise unable to be fully Korean in South Korea or in the Korean diaspora. For another young French adoptee who declared 'I don't like France and I don't like Korea,' the question still remains, Where can I go?"[41]

Yet it is in the imagined community of The Gathering that Kim finds the potentially radical political solution to feelings of "homelessness" described by Lifton as well as by the Korean adoptees. Homelessness is a current that runs through much adoption literature, irrespective of whether adoption involves actual dislocation from a specific country. Lifton describes herself as homeless, and indeed, her comfort in "Asian cultures," she attributes to her status as an adoptee. Lifton's experience shows how deeply heterosexual kinship is bound up with national belonging. Hence the Korean adoptees' sense that they do not belong in South Korea because they do not have a family history in the traditional Korean sense. But is holding onto this homelessness an expression of melancholia? Here again, we are returned to Eng and Han's insightful essay. Their whole point is that melancholia may be the only available psychic response to the erasure of the uniqueness of the narratable self. But events like The Gathering open the political space for mourning and for repairing the conditions of belonging that Korean adoptees can claim as their own.

As parents, we all have to mourn our children as they travel into worlds where we cannot follow them. For adopting parents, this is often painfully obvious. White parents were not invited to The Gathering. They were not offered the chance by the South Korean government to "marry" South Korea, nor are they called by their position in society to negotiate the multiple meanings of what it means to be Korean. The effort of some parents to hold onto their children results from these parents thinking that their children are not actually their own. Parenting involves the acceptance that a child never belongs to the parent. With this acceptance, adopting parents will be able to let their children return to the worlds from which they hailed and enter new worlds they create with others out of "gatherings." Although Lifton is particularly sensitive to the plight of transnational and transracially adopted children, she fails to fully address the other scene of mourning that haunts transnational adoptions. At the time I adopted my daughter, I believed myself to hold no illusions about the role of the United States in South America. But the full ethical and political ambiguity did not hit me until I stood on that balcony in Paraguay. There it was: in 1993, there was no way for an adoption from Paraguay to the United States to be just. I mourned for a just world. After I went home, I supported the Paraguayan government in their effort to suspend adoption. To mourn for a just world does not mean to immerse oneself in guilt or the self-beratement of melancholia. But it does mean that adopting parents are called to recognize the injustice of the closed system of adoption, to make their own reparations, starting with making that injustice part of the story of adoption.[1] Gabriella Delgado Barrio did not give up her daughter because I was destined to raise her. She gave her up because she could not be a single mother in the Paraguay of her time. In the story and image of Gabriella I give my daughter, I imagine a woman who courageously faced the worst odds and obstacles. If we deny the conditions in which the other mother gave up her child, we fail to recognize the injustice of those conditions, along with the uniqueness of our adopted child's narratable self and her relationship to us. As a matter of reparations and indebtedness, mourning for justice is the very least we owe our adopted children. For only through that mourning may we be able to join them in dreaming up new family stories.

References

CHAPTER 1

1. "Smoking Baghdad," *The New York Post*, March 22, 2003.
2. Nuha Al-Radi, *Baghdad Diaries: A Woman's Chronicle of War and Exile* (New York: Vintage Books, 2003), 11.
3. Ibid., 13.
4. Ibid., 27.
5. Ibid., 29.
6. Ibid., 29.
7. Ibid., 36–37.
8. Ibid., 38.
9. Ibid., 43–44.
10. Ibid., 47.
11. Ibid., 40.
12. Ibid., 41.
13. Elshtain, *Women and War*, 152.
14. Richard Falk, *The Great Terror War* (New York: Olive Branch Press, 2003), 125.
15. Elshtain, *Women and War*, 265.
16. Jean Bethke Elshtain, *Just War Against Terror* (New York: Basic Books, 2003), 87–88.
17. Cited in Arundathi Roy, *Power Politics* (Cambridge: South End Press, 2001), 111.
18. Nuha Al-Radi, *Baghdad Diaries: A Woman's Chronicle of War and Exile* (New York: Vintage Books, 2003), 93.
19. Ibid., 67.
20. Arundathi Roy, "Mesopotamia. Babylon. The Tigris and Euphrates," www.outlookindia.com, April 2, 2003.
21. Elshtain, *Just War Against Terror*, 144.

22. See Tariq Ali, *The Clash of Fundamentalisms: Crusades, Jihads, and Modernity* (London: Verso, 2002), 74–78.
23. Michael Dobbs, "US Had Key Role in Iraq Build Up," *The Washington Post*, December 30, 2002.
24. Lawrence Lapham, *Theater of War* (New York: New Press, 2002), 158.
25. Ronald Dworkin, "The Trouble with Tribunals," *NY Review of Books*, April 5, 2002, and Ronald Dworkin, "The Threat to Patriotism," *NY Review of Books*, February 28, 2002.
26. Cited in Jean Bethke Elshtain, *Just War Against Terror* (New York: Basic Books, 2003), 92.
27. Elshtain, *Just War Against Terror*, 184.
28. Ibid., 82.
29. Étienne Balibar, *Politics and the Other Scene*, trans. Christine Jones, James Swenson, and Chris Turner (London: Verso, 2002), 144.
30. Elshtain, *Women and War*, 258.
31. Carolin Emcke, "War on Terrorism and the Crises of the Political," in *The Ethics of Terrorism and Counter-Terrorism*, Ed. Georg Meggle, forthcoming.
32. Elshtain, *Just War Against Terror*, 193.
33. Tariq Ali, *The Clash of Fundamentalisms: Crusades, Jihads, and Modernity* (London: Verso, 2002), 74.
34. Elshtain, *Just War Against Terror*, 41.
35. Ibid., 142.
36. Ibid., 141.
37. Ibid., 86.
38. Ali, *The Clash of Fundamentalisms: Crusades, Jihads, and Modernity*, 312–313.
39. Daniel Bergner, "Where the Enemy Is Everywhere and Nowhere," *New York Times Magazine*, July 20, 2003, 40–41.
40. Richard Falk, "Humanitarian Intervention: A Forum," *The Nation*, July 18, 2003.
41. Elshtain, *Women and War*, 157.

CHAPTER 2

1. Richard Falk, "Defining a Just War." *The Nation*, October 29, 2001, 11.
2. Ibid., 11.
3. Richard Falk, *The Great Terror War* (New York, Northampton: Olive Branch Press, 2003), 64–65.
4. Ibid., 8.
5. Ibid., 9–10.
6. Ibid., 9.
7. Ibid., xxi.
8. Falk, "Defining a Just War." 12.
9. Ibid., 12.
10. Ibid., 15.
11. Richard Falk, "A Just Response," *The Nation*, October 8, 2001, 2.
12. Falk, *The Great Terror War*, 69.
13. Ibid., 68.
14. Ibid., 69.
15. Ibid., 183.
16. Ibid., 10–11.

17. Jonathan Schell, *The Unconquerable World: Power, Nonviolence, and the Will of the People* (New York: Metropolitan Books, 2003), 365.
18. Falk, *The Great Terror War*, 29–30.
19. Ibid., 81.
20. Richard Falk, *Explorations of at the Edge of Time. The Prospects for World Order* (Philadelphia, PA: Temple University Press, 1993), 15.
21. Ibid., 16.
22. Etienne Balibar, *Politics and the Other Scene* (London, New York: Verso, 2002), 29–30.
23. Michael Walzer, *Just and Unjust Wars. A Moral Argument with Historical Illustrations.* (New York: Basic Books, 1992).
24. Schell, *The Unconquerable World: Power, Nonviolence, and the Will of the People*, 2003, 355.
25. Immanuel Kant, "Toward Perpetual Peace," in *Practical Philosophy, The Cambridge Edition of Immanuel Kant*, Ed. Mary J. Gregor (Cambride: Cambride University Press, 1999), 319.
26. Immanuel Kant, "Toward Perpetual Peace," 317, 322, 325–326.
27. Claude Lefort, "The Idea of Humanity and the Project of Universal Peace," *Writing: The Political Test*, trans. David Ames Curtis (Durham, NC: Duke University Press, 2000), 157.
28. Ibid., 157.

CHAPTER 3

1. Throughout this essay, I primarily rely on Rawls' monograph published in 1999. However, in several cases where I thought his initial formulation was more succinct, I have relied on the original essay published in *Collected Papers*, Samuel Freeman, Ed. (Cambridge, MA: Harvard University Press, 1999), 529–564.
2. John Rawls, *The Law of Peoples* (Cambridge, MA: Harvard University Press, 1999), 11–12.
3. Ibid., 21.
4. Ibid., 22.
5. Ibid., 75.
6. Ibid., 30–31.
7. John Rawls, "The Law of Peoples," Collected Papers, Ed. Samuel Freeman (Cambridge, MA: Harvard University Press, 1999), 535–536.
8. Rawls, *The Law of Peoples*, 11–12.
9. Ibid, 59.
10. Rawls, "The Law of Peoples," 547.
11. Rawls, *The Law of Peoples*, 33.
12. Ibid., 37.
13. Rawls, *The Law of Peoples*, 26–27.
14. John Rawls, *A Theory of Justice* (Cambridge: Belknap Press, 1999), 514.
15. John Rawls, "Fifty Years after Hiroshima," *Collected Papers*, Ed. Samuel Freeman (Cambridge, MA: Harvard University Press, 1999), 572.
16. Rawls, *A Theory of Justice*, 325.
17. Arundathi Roy, *War Talk* (Cambridge: South End Press, 2003), 13.
18. Rawls, *The Law of Peoples*, 75–76.
19. Ibid., 76–77.
20. Ibid., 73.

21. John Rawls, "The Idea of Public Reason Revisited," *Collected Papers*, Ed. Samuel Freeman (Cambridge, MA: Harvard University Press, 1999), 594.
22. Rawls, *The Law of Peoples*, 80.
23. Rawls, "The Law of Peoples," 556.
24. Rawls, *The Law of Peoples*, 109.
25. Rawls, "The Law of Peoples," 559.
26. Rawls, *The Law of Peoples*, 111.
27. See Leif Weinar, "The Legitimacy of Peoples," *Global Justice and Transnational Politics: Essays on the Moral and Political Challenges of Globalization*, Eds. Pablo De Greiff and Ciaran Cronin (Cambridge, MA: MIT Press, 2002).
28. Rawls, "The Law of Peoples," 560.
29. Rawls, *The Law of Peoples*, 85.
30. Thomas Pogge, "Human Rights and Human Responsibilities," *Global Justice and Transnational Politics: Essays on the Moral and Political Challenges of Globalization*, Eds. Pablo De Greiff and Ciaran Cronin (Cambridge, MA: MIT Press, 2002), 165.
31. Ibid., 164.
32. Ibid., 172.
33. Amartya Sen, *Development as Freedom* (New York: Knopf, 1999), 230.
34. Amartya Sen, "Justice across Borders," *Global Justice and Transnational Politics: Essays on the Moral and Political Challenges of Globalization*, Eds. Pablo De Greiff and Ciaran Cronin (Cambridge, MA: MIT Press, 2002), 41.
35. Ibid., 43.

CHAPTER 4

1. Amartya Sen, "Equality of What," *The Tanner Lectures on Human Values Volume 7*, Ed. Sterling McMurrin (Salt Lake City: University of Utah Press, 1986), 215–216.
2. Ibid., 218.
3. Ibid., 218.
4. Ronald Dworkin, "Do Liberty and Equality Conflict?," *Living as Equals*, Ed. Paul Barker (Oxford: Oxford University Press, 1996), 45.
5. Amartya Sen, *Inequality Reexamined* (Cambridge, MA: Harvard University Press, 1992), 40–41.
6. Ibid., 49.
7. Amartya Sen, *Development as Freedom* (New York: Knopf, 1999), 18.
8. Ibid., 15.
9. Ibid., 18–19.
10. Ibid., 19.
11. Ibid.
12. Ibid., 142.
13. Ibid., 39–40.
14. Ibid., 40.
15. Ibid., 33.
16. Ibid.
17. Ibid.
18. Ibid., 82.
19. Ibid.
20. Ibid.

21. Amartya Sen, "The Many Faces of Gender Inequality," *New Republic*, Vol. 225, No.12, September 17, 2001, 35–36.
22. Ibid., 39.
23. Ibid., 40.
24. Sen, *Development as Freedom*, 82.
25. Ibid., 83.
26. Ibid.
27. Ibid., 76.
28. Ibid.
29. Ibid., 31–32.
30. Martha Nussbaum, *Women and Human Development: The Capabilities Approach* (Cambridge, MA: Cambridge University Press, 2000), 72–73.
31. Sen, *Inequality Reexamined*, 31.
32. Nussbaum, *Women and Human Development: The Capabilities Approach*, 13.
33. Jane Flax, "On Encountering Incommensurability: Martha Nussbaum's Aristotelian Practice," *Controversies in Feminism*, Ed. James Sterba (Oxford: Rowan and Littlefield Publishers, 2001), 38.
34. Nussbaum, *Women and Human Development: The Capabilities Approach*, 120.
35. Ibid., 48.
36. Ibid., 50.
37. John Rawls, "Law of Peoples," *Collected Papers*, Ed. Samuel Freeman (Cambridge, MA: Harvard University Press, 1999), 551–552.
38. Nussbaum, *Women and Human Development: The Capabilities Approach*, 55.
39. Amartya Sen, "Justice Across Borders," *Global Justice and Transnational Politics: Essays on the Moral and Political Challenges of Globalization*, Eds. Pablo De Greiff and Ciaran Cronin (Cambridge, MA: MIT Press, 2002), 40.
40. Ibid., 50.
41. Ibid., 42.
42. Ibid., 41.
43. Étienne Balibar, *Politics and the Other Scene*, trans. Christine Jones, James Swenson, and Chris Turner (New York: Verso, 2002), 160.
44. Ibid., 150–151.
45. Ibid., 29–30.

CHAPTER 5

1. Theodor W. Adorno, "Progress," *Critical Models*, trans. Henry Pickford (New York: Columbia University Press, 1998), 143–144.
2. Étienne Balibar, *Politics and the Other Scene*, trans. Christine Jones, James Swenson, and Chris Turner (New York: Verso, 2002), 137.
3. Ernesto Laclau, "Identity and Hegemony," *Contingency, Hegemony, Universality* with Judith Butler and Slavoj Zizek (London: Verso, 2000), 81.
4. I borrow this understanding of equality and liberty from my colleague Gordon Schochet.
5. Interview by "Move On" (on file with the author).
6. Edward Rothstein, "Left Has Hard Time in Era of Terrorism," *The New York Times*, (December 21, 2002), 11.
7. Former "Immigration and Naturalization Service," which has been integrated into the Department of Homeland Security.
8. Richard Rorty, *Philosophy and Social Hope* (New York: Penguin Putnam Inc., 1999).

9. Adorno, "Progress," 153.
10. Ibid.
11. Jay Bernstein, *Adorno: Disenchantment and Ethics* (Cambridge: Cambridge University Press, 2001), 68.
12. Adorno, "Progress," 152.
13. Ibid., 144.
14. Ibid., 152.
15. Indeed in his essay on progress, Adorno disagrees with some of his earlier critical readings of Hegel; thus he writes that "Hegel as well as Marx bore witness to the fact that even the dialectical view of progress needs correction . . . It may be more than mere coincidence that Hegel, despite his famous definition of history, has no detailed theory of progress and that Marx himself seems to have avoided the word." Adorno, "Progress," 144.
16. Immanuel Kant, "Idea for a Universal History with a Cosmopolitan Purpose," *Political Writings*, ed. H.S. Reiss and trans. H.B. Nisbet (Cambridge: Cambridge University Press, 1991), 47.
17. Adorno, "Progress," 154.
18. Balibar, *Politics and the Other Scene*, 157.
19. Adorno, "Progress," 153.
20. Ibid., 150.
21. Ibid., 153.
22. Immanuel Kant, "Metaphysics of Morals," *Practical Philosophy*, ed. and trans. Mary Gregor (Cambridge: Cambridge University Press, 1996), 534 (emphasis mine).
23. Adorno, "Progress," 69–70.

CHAPTER 6

1. Janelle Brown, *Ms.*, "Coalition of Hope," Spring 2002, 65–76.
2. Unpublished e-mail correspondence on file with the author.
3. Giorgio Agamben, "Beyond Human Rights," *Means Without End: Notes on Politics*, trans. Cesare Cesarino (Minneapolis: University of Minnesota Press, 2000), 22.
4. Anne E. Brodsky, *With All Our Strength: The Revolutionary Association of the Women of Afghanistan* (New York: Routledge, 2003), 200.
5. Ibid., 273.
6. Ibid., 272.
7. Ibid., xi–xii.
8. Ibid., 152.
9. Gayatri Spivak, "Righting Wrongs," in *Human Rights, Human Wrongs: The Oxford Amnesty Lectures 2001*, Ed. Nicholas Owen (New York: Oxford University Press, 2003), 205–206.
10. Ibid., 227.
11. See generally, Martha Nussbaum, *Women and Human Development: The Capabilities Approach* (Cambridge: Cambridge University Press, 2000).
12. See generally, Amartya Sen, *Development as Freedom* (New York: Knopf, 1999).
13. Ibid., 229–230.

14. See Suad Joseph, "Women Between Nation and State in Lebanon," in *Between Woman and Nation: Nationalisms, Feminisms, and the State*, Eds. Caren Kaplan, Norma Alarcón, and Minoo Moallem (Durham and London: Duke University Press, 1999), 162–181.

15. See Benedict Anderson, *Imagined Communities* (London: Verso, 1983).

16. Laura Elisa Pérez, "El desorden, Nationalism, and Chicana/o Aesthetics," in *Between Woman and Nation: Nationalisms, Feminisms, and the State*, eds. Caren Kaplan, Norma Alarcón, and Minoo Moallem (Durham and London: Duke University Press, 1999, 19–46.

17. Ibid., 28.

18. Ibid., 29.

19. Norma Alarcón, "Chicana Feminism: In the Tracks of "The" Native Woman," in *Between Woman and Nation: Nationalisms, Feminisms, and the State*, Eds. Caren Kaplan, Norma Alarcón, and Minoo Moallem (Durham and London: Duke University Press, 1999), 66–67.

20. *Women for Peace* (Belgrade, 2001), 13.

21. *Women for Peace* (Belgrade, 2001), 17.

22. See Martha Nussbaum, *Upheavals of Thought: The Intelligence of the Emotions* (New York: Cambridge University Press, 2001).

23. Ibid., 501.

24. Jacques Derrida, *Negotiations*, trans. Elizabeth Rottenberg (Stanford: Stanford University Press, 2002), 324–325.

25. *Women for Peace* (Belgrade, 2001), 148.

26. Yoko Fukumura and Martha Matsuoka, "Redefining Security: Okinawa Women's Resistance to U.S. Militarism," in *Women's Activism and Globalization: Linking Local Struggles and Transnational Politics*, Eds. Nancy A. Naples and Manisha Desai (New York: Routledge, 2002), 240.

CHAPTER 7

1. The former INS has been integrated into the Department of Homeland Security.

2. Diane J. Schemo, "Adoption in Paraguay: Mothers Cry Theft," *The New York Times* on the web, (March 18, 1996).

3. Rita J. Simon and Howard Altstein, *Adoption Across Borders* (Lanham, MD: Rowman & Littlefield), 33.

4. Aihwa Ong, *Flexible Citizenship: The Cultural Logics of Transnationality* (Durham, N.C.: Duke University Press, 1999), 2.

5. Betty J. Lifton, *Journey of the Adopted Self: A Quest for Wholeness* (New York: Basic Books, 1995), 24.

6. Betty J. Lifton, *Twice Born: Memoirs of an Adopted Daughter* (New York: St. Martin's Griffin), 255.

7. Lifton, *Journey of the Adopted Self*, 36–37.

8. Ibid., 11.

9. Lifton, *Twice Born*, 15.

10. Sigmund Freud, "Mourning and Melancholia" in *Collected Papers Volume IV: Papers on Metapsychology* (New York: Basic Books), 153

11. Lifton, *Twice Born*, 5.

12. Freud, "Mourning and Melancholia," 155.

13. Ibid., 159.

14. Lifton, *Twice Born*, 7.
15. Ibid., 10–11.
16. Ibid., 11.
17. Melanie Klein, *Love, Guilt, and Reparation and Other Works 1921–1945* (New York: Free Press, 1984), 312.
18. Ibid., 362.
19. Ibid., 369.
20. Lifton, *Twice Born*, 140.
21. Adriana Caverero, *Relating Narratives: Storytelling and Selfhood*, trans. Paul A. Kottman (New York: Routledge, 2000), 11.
22. Ibid., 89.
23. Ibid., 39.
24. Ibid., 39.
25. Ibid., 72.
26. Ibid., 19.
27. Lifton, *Twice Born*, 101.
28. Ibid., 258.
29. Ibid., 170.
30. Ibid., 225–226.
31. Sanchez-Pardo, *Cultures of the Death Drive: Melanie Klein and Modernist Melancholia* (Durham, NC: Duke University Press, 2003), 131.
32. Nancy Verrier, *The Primal Wound: Understanding the Adopted Child* (Nancy Verrier, 1993), 16.
33. Sanchez-Pardo, *Cultures of the Death Drive*, 137.
34. Ibid., 69.
35. David L. Eng and Shinhee Han, "A Dialogue on Racial Melancholia," in *Loss: The Politics of Mourning*, Eds. David L. Eng and David Kazanjian (California: The University of California Press, 2002), 351.
36. Eleana Kim, "Wedding Citizenship and Culture: Korean Adoptees and the Global Family of Korea," *Social Text*, Vol. 21, No. 1, Eds. Toby Volkman and Cindy Katz, (Durham, NC: Duke University Press, March 2003), 63.
37. Ibid., 61.
38. Ibid., 66.
39. Ibid., 71.
40. Ibid., 67.
41. Ibid., 75.

Bibliography

Adorno, Theodor. "Progress." *Critical Models.* Trans. Henry Pickford. New York: Columbia University Press, 1998.

Agamben, Giorgio. *Means Without End: Notes on Politics.* Translated by Cesare Cesarino. Minneapolis: University of Minnesota Press, 2000.

Alarcón, Norma. "Chicana Feminism: In the Tracks of 'The' Native Woman." In Caren Kaplan, Norma Alarcón, and Minoo Moallem, eds., *Between Woman and Nation: Nationalisms, Transnational feminisms, and the State.* Durham: Duke University Press, 1999.

Anderson, Benedict. *Imagined Communities.* London: Verso, 1983.

Balibar, Étienne. *Politics and the Other Scene.* Trans. Christine Jones, James Swenson, and Chris Turner. London, New York: Verso, 2002.

Bernstein, Jay. *Adorno: Disenchantment and Ethics.* Cambridge: Cambridge University Press, 2001.

Brodsky, Anne E. *With All Our Strength: The Revolutionary Association of the Women of Afghanistan.* New York: Routledge, 2003.

Janelle Brown, "Coalition of Hope," *Ms.*, Spring 2002: 65–76.

Caverero, Adriana. *Relating Narratives: Storytelling and Selfhood.* Trans. Paul A. Kottman. New York: Routledge, 2000.

Derrida, Jacques. *Negotiations.* Trans. Peggy Kamuf. Stanford: Stanford University Press, 2002.

Dworkin, Ronald. "Do Liberty and Equality Conflict?" In Paul Barker, ed., *Living as Equals.* Oxford: Oxford University Press, 1996.

Eng, David L. and Shinhee Han. "A Dialogue on Racial Melancholia." In David Eng and David Kazanjian, eds., *Loss: The Politics of Mourning.* California: The University of California Press, 2002.

Falk, Richard. *The Great Terror War.* Gloucestershire: Arris Publishing Ltd., 2003.

Falk, Richard. "Defining a Just War." *The Nation*, vol. 273, no. 13, October 29, 2001: 11–16.

Falk, Richard. *Explorations of at the Edge of Time.* Philadelphia: Temple University Press, 1993.

Flax, Jane. "On Encountering Incommensurability: Martha Nussbaum's Aristotelian Practice." In James Sterba, ed., *Controversies in Feminism*. Oxford: Rowan and Littlefield Publishers, 2001.

Freud, Sigmund. "Mourning and Melancholia." In *Collected Papers Volume IV: Papers on Metapsychology*. New York: Basic Books, 1959.

Fukumura, Yoko and Martha Matsuoka. "Redefining Security: Okinawa Women's Resistance to U.S. Militarism." In Nancy A. Naples and Manisha Desai, eds., *Women's Activism and Globalization: Linking Local Struggles and Transnational Politics*. New York: Routledge, 2002.

Hobbes, Thomas. *Leviathan*. Ed. Edwin Curley. Indianapolis: Hackett Publishing Company, 1994.

Joseph, Suad. "Women Between Nation and State in Lebanon." In Caren Kaplan, Norma Alarcón, and Minoo Moallem, eds., *Between Woman and Nation: Nationalisms, Transnational Feminisms, and the State*. Durham: Duke University Press, 1999.

Kant, Immanuel. "Metaphysics of Morals." In Mary Gregor, ed., *Practical Philosophy*. Cambridge: Cambridge University Press, 1996.

Kant, Immanuel. "Toward Perpetual Peace." In Mary Gregor, ed., *Practical Philosophy*. Cambridge: Cambridge University Press, 1996.

Kant, Immanuel. "Idea for a Universal History with a Cosmopolitan Purpose." *Political Writings*. Ed. H.S. Reiss and trans. H.B. Nisbet. Cambridge: Cambridge University Press, 1991.

Kim, Eleana. "Wedding Citizenship and Culture: Korean Adoptees and the Global Family of Korea." *Social Text*, Spring 2003, vol. 21, no. 1: 57–82.

Klein, Melanie. *Love, Guilt, and Reparation and Other Works 1921–1945*. New York: Free Press, 1984.

Laclau, Ernesto. "Identity and Hegemony." In Ernesto Laclau, Judith Butler, and Slavoj Zizek, *Contingency, Hegemony, Universality*. London: Verso, 2000.

Lefort, Claude. "The Idea of Humanity and the Project of Universal Peace." *Writing: The Political Test*. Trans. David Ames Curtis. Durham: Duke University Press, 2000.

Lifton, Betty J. *Journey of the Adopted Self: A Quest for Wholeness*. New York: Basic Books, 1995.

Lifton, Betty J. *Twice Born: Memoirs of an Adopted Daughter*. New York: McGraw Hill, 1975.

Nussbaum, Martha. *Upheavals of Thought: The Intelligence of the Emotions*. New York: Cambridge University Press, 2001.

Nussbaum, Martha. *Women and Human Development: The Capabilities Approach*. Cambridge: Cambridge University Press, 2000.

Ong, Aihwa. *Flexible Citizenship: The Cultural Logics of Transnationality*. Durham: Duke University Press, 1999.

Pérez, Laura Elisa. "El desorden, Nationalism, and Chicana/o Aesthetics." In Caren Kaplan, Norma Alarcón, and Minoo Moallem, eds., *Between Woman and Nation: Nationalisms, Transnational feminisms, and the State*. Durham: Duke University Press, 1999.

Pogge, Thomas. "Human Rights and Human Responsibilities." In Pablo De Greiff and Ciaran Cronin, eds., *Global Justice and Transnational Politics: Essays on the Moral and Political Challenges of Globalization*. Cambridge: MIT Press, 2002.

Rawls, John. *A Theory of Justice*. Cambridge: Belknap Press, 1999.

Rawls, John. "Law of Peoples." In Samuel Freeman, ed., *Collected Papers*. Cambridge: Harvard University Press, 1999.

Rawls, John. "Fifty Years after Hiroshima." In Samuel Freeman, ed., *Collected Papers*. Cambridge: Harvard University Press, 1999.

Rawls, John. "The Idea of Public Reason Revisited." In Samuel Freeman, ed., *Collected Papers*. Cambridge: Harvard University Press, 1999.

Roy, Arundathi. *War Talk*. Cambridge: South End Press, 2003.

Sanchez-Pardo, Esther. *Cultures of the Death Drive: Melanie Klein and Modernist Melancholia*. Durham: Duke University Press, 2003.

Schell, Jonathan. *The Unconquerable World: Power, Nonviolence, and the Will of the People*. New York: Metropolitan Books, 2003.

Schemo, Diane J. *Adoption in Paraguay: Mothers Cry Theft*. The New York Times on the web, (March 18, 1996).

Sen, Amartya. "Justice across Borders." In Pablo De Greiff and Ciaran Cronin, eds., *Global Justice and Transnational Politics: Essays on the Moral and Political Challenges of Globalization*. Cambridge: MIT Press, 2002.

Sen, Amartya. "The Many Faces of Gender Inequality." *New Republic*, vol. 225, no. 12, September 17, 2001: 35–41.

Sen, Amartya. *Development as Freedom*. New York: Knopf, 1999.

Sen, Amartya. *Inequality Reexamined*. Cambridge: Harvard University Press, 1992.

Sen, Amartya. "Equality of What?" In Sterling McMurrin, ed., *The Tanner Lectures on Human Values Volume 7*. Salt Lake City: University of Utah Press, 1986.

Simon, Rita J. and Howard Altstein. *Adoption Across Borders*. Lanham: Rowan & Littlefield.

Spivak, Gayatri. "Righting Wrongs." In Nicholas Owen, ed., *Human Rights, Human Wrongs: The Oxford Amnesty Lectures 2001*. New York: Oxford University Press, 2003.

Verrier, Nancy. *The Primal Wound: Understanding the Adopted Child*. Nancy Verrier, 1993.

Women for Peace (Belgrade: 2001).

Index